Fitness for Purpose

Fitness for Purpose

Edited by Dorma Urwin

Essays in Higher Education

by Christopher Ball

The Society for Research
into Higher Education
& NFER-NELSON

Chapters 1, 2, 3, 5, 7, 9, 13, 15, 18 and 19 are drawn from papers that first appeared in the Keble College *Record* 1980, *The Times Literary Supplement* 31 January 1981, the Thames Polytechnic Annual Lecture series 1981, *The Arts and Higher Education* edited by Ken Robinson (SRHE 1982), *Oxford Review of Education* 8 (3) 1982, *Economies of Scale in Higher Education* edited by Sinclair Goodlad (SRHE 1983), *The Future for Higher Education* edited by David Jacques and John Richardson (SRHE & NFER-NELSON 1984), the Association of Colleges for Further and Higher Education (ACFHE) Annual General Meeting series 1984, *Oxford Review of Education* 11 (1) 1985, and the Manchester Polytechnic Report of a conference held at the Centre for Educational Development and Training (FE/HE) 30 October 1984.

They are adapted and reproduced here by kind agreement with the editors and copyright holders.

Cover illustration by David Smith by kind permission of *The Times Higher Education Supplement*.

Published by SRHE & NFER-NELSON
At the University, Guildford, Surrey GU2 5XH

First published 1985
© Christoper Ball

ISBN 1-85059-15 X
Code 8945 021

Typeset by FD Graphics, Fleet, Hampshire.
Printed and bound in Great Britain by Billing & Sons Ltd., Worcester.

Preface

Like Autolycus, I am something of a magpie — at least, as far as my reading is concerned. And so I readily acknowledge at the outset a general debt to all the many unacknowledged sources of ideas, themes, references, quotations, phrases and figures in these essays. (The errors are mine alone.) In particular, I am grateful to all my colleagues at Keble, Oxford, and NAB for their constructive advice and criticism, most especially to Geoffrey Rowell and Ruth Lawrence, Harry Judge, Chelly Halsey and Dick Smethurst, and to John Bevan and Leslie Wagner. I also thank my wife and family for their patience and encouragement over many years. Finally, I offer my heartfelt thanks to Sally Kington of the Society for Research into Higher Education, whose skills have made the publication of this book seem quite trouble-free and simple and to Dorma Urwin, colleague and friend for some seven years at both CNAA and NAB, whose advice, support and care in the preparation and editing of this book have been to me of untold value.

For my Brother

Contents

Introduction

'I have been a selfish being all my life, in practice, though not in principle' (Jane Austen, *Pride and Prejudice*). Mr Darcy's confession to Elizabeth Bennett is an appropriate starting point for this collection of essays and addresses in education. For the education in question was, first of all and continuingly so, my own. Five years ago I became aware of a certain uneasiness about higher education as I understood it and practised it. The phrase 'tyranny of scholarship' summed up my concern at that time – concern that we might have dangerously narrowed the purposes of advanced education by conforming them too closely to the values of scholarship and the prevailing research ethos. Such a generalization may strike many as rash or absurd. Neither a university college nor a polytechnic offers an education which can be so conveniently and dismissively summarized. And yet, I remain uneasy about the dislocation which often exists between our students' experience of higher education and their actual lives after graduation. I believe that our courses are still too strongly influenced by the (false) assumption that many of our students will find research posts or become 'dons' – too rarely designed to provide an appropriate preparation for the real lives ahead of them. In saying this, I am not calling for any principle of naïve relevance in higher education. Some of the wiser employers tell us that they are seeking young people who have learned (above all) how to learn, and whose confidence and hopes are unimpaired. That formulation seems to me a ringing challenge to our educational system – and to my own teaching.

If the idea of the 'tyranny of scholarship' provided a point of departure for this book, the phrase which summarizes its provisional conclusion (and which I have borrowed from Sir Keith Joseph) is 'fitness for purpose'. Unless we are prepared to define – and redefine – the purposes of our courses, our research, our institutions, our phases and systems of education, we shall fail to find any secure basis for evaluating them. This book does not pretend to offer any thoroughgoing or complete redefinition of educational purpose: it does no more than pose the question and suggest some lines of inquiry which might lead others to satisfactory answers. But I hold firm to the idea that we shall most certainly strengthen the educational service (of which higher education is but a part), not primarily by securing greater resources for it, or improving its status and morale, or changing its government or its institutions (important though these things are), but rather by addressing the issue of fitness for purpose. What is education for? What are the purposes of higher education? And how far does the educational service match and respond to and fulfil those purposes?

A little more than five years ago I was Tutor in English Language, and Bursar, at Lincoln College, Oxford. I was always curious about other forms of higher education, other institutions, other ways of teaching my subject, and from time to time during the 1960s and 1970s became external examiner at a range of universities in Scotland and England, and served on several subject boards of the Council for National Academic Awards. In 1980 I became Warden of Keble College, Oxford, and in 1982 Chairman of the Board of the then National Advisory Body for Local Authority Higher Education (NAB, and now for Public Sector Higher Education). Few people have had such a rich opportunity for reflection upon, and action in, the various realms of higher education – college, university, nation. It has been a challenging and exhilarating period. This book contains a (partial and personal) record of that time. In rereading it I see that some things are inconsistent, some things unclear, and some things perhaps indefensible. But what was said was said. To those who have been puzzled or offended by my words, I apologize – reminding them of Elizabeth's reply to Darcy: 'My manners must have been at fault, but not intentionally I assure you. I never meant to deceive you, but my spirits might often lead me wrong.'

1

The Pursuit of Truth

'On the bitterly cold evening of Sunday, 20 January, 1980 (on which a cloudless sky happily revealed the old moon cradled in the young moon's arms)' — in the words of the editor of the College Record — I was installed as ninth Warden of Keble, and first addressed the assembled college in the chapel. Although I had spent half my life in Oxford, I knew little of my new college. Oxford colleges are private and modest institutions on the whole, and not easily known from without. What the public thinks it sees is often more a caricature than the true character. I knew Keble to be a large college with a strong Anglican tradition (I am the first lay Warden) and, in comparison with other Oxford colleges, a recent foundation and poorly-endowed. All this attracted me: I wanted to be where there was a sense of purpose and some work to be done (see Appendix D). And I wished at the outset to stress the idea of the college as a place of education and learning — not a mere hostel for undergraduates or dining club for dons. But it is also a community: five years later, with much done and more still to do, I am conscious above all of the collegial values of Keble, and of Oxford, and understand better now what I meant then in quoting (and often repeating) Langland's words: 'Learn to love, and leave all other'.

This is not an easy age to be serious in: 'The best lack all conviction, while the worst are full of passionate intensity'. The Victorians knew how to be serious, and were not embarrassed by the expression of noble sentiments in appropriate language. For example, John Keble's poem for the second Sunday after Epiphany (today) meditating on the miracle of the wedding feast at Cana ends thus:

> Nor shall dull age, as worldlings say,
>   The heavenward flame annoy:
> The Saviour cannot pass away,
>   And with him lives our joy.
>
> Ever the richest tenderest glow
>   Sets round th' autumnal sun —
> But there sight fails: no heart may know
>   The bliss when life is done.

Such is thy banquet, dearest Lord:
   O give us grace, to cast
Our lot with thine, to trust thy word,
   And keep our best till last.

How far from us seem such thoughts, with their simple certainty, and such words, direct and unselfconscious! We, too readily, suspect rhetoric, and thereby sacrifice nobility of statement; we fear to seem hypocritical, and therefore take refuge in an all-enveloping irony; we are afraid of authority (our own and others') and thus mislay the concept of responsibility. The Victorian taboos — their avoidance, for example, of direct reference to physical love — we have boldly destroyed; but no one notices that in their place we have erected a new and extensive network of taboos — we are too often and too easily ashamed to speak seriously about serious things; and words like *faith* and *truth* become obsolescent, or are used only in specialized senses.

'The Warden shall endeavour' — so the college's fifth Statute lays down — 'he shall endeavour to the best of his ability to further the interests of the College as a place wherein education and learning shall be promoted and the free exercise of religion permitted and protected. In the exercise of his functions as defined by these Statutes he shall have due regard to the established traditions of the College.'

Traditions change — though on the whole it is best and right when they change slowly; institutions, like plants or families or languages, are damaged by abrupt change, but like languages, families or plants, they die if no change takes place at all. In its one hundred and ten years' history, this college has changed gradually, continually and remarkably; listen to the Preamble to the Statutes, which reminds us of the ideas of our founders:

> Keble College was founded in 1870 in memory of the Reverend John Keble, on land in the parish of St.Giles purchased from the President and Scholars of St.John's College, with the object of providing a University education for young men in a College conducted in accordance with the principles of the Church of England.

A jarring paragraph, surely; full of mild shocks for the contemporary reader. One notes and reflects on the phrases 'young men' and 'the principles of the Church of England'. The old Statutes (II clause 3) stated clearly but brutally, 'No woman shall be a member of the College'. I welcome the college's decision — fulfilled by the first mixed intake last October — to admit women as members of the college, look forward to the gradual development of a fully mixed college, and believe that Keble will more readily be 'a place wherein education and learning may be promoted' if both sexes are free to apply for membership and compete for appointments.

I also welcome the change from the apparently restrictive requirement that the education must be conducted in accordance with the principles of the Church of England to the liberal provision that ' the free exercise of religion is to be permitted and protected'. Though, in saying that, I am conscious that the college (if it is wise) will continue in the future, as in the past, to draw inspiration and guidance from the teachings of Christ, as interpreted by the English Church. The chapel, like the library and the Hall, is open to all, and offers spiritual nourishment to complement the physical and intellectual nourishment provided by the Hall and library; if you can eat better elsewhere, by all means do so: but do not make the mistake of believing that mankind can do without spiritual nourishment altogether.

The college, then, has two central objects or aims: the promotion of education and learning, and the protection of the free exercise of religion. Although at first glance these seem to be two very different aims, they are not inconsistent: reflection will show that they can be reconciled and even united, as in the instruction given to the Dreamer by Holy Church (portrayed as a lovely but rather overbearing lady) in Langland's great poem *Piers Plowman*: she tells Will, the Dreamer: 'When all treasures are tried, Truth is the best'. It is this profoundly simple and profoundly difficult affirmation that this college (that *any* college) exists to teach and to explore.

Simone Weill, the French mystic, expressed a similar idea in the language of the twentieth century when she paradoxically asserted that if the pursuit of truth led us away from the teachings of Christ, then Christ would want us to follow the truth. After all, we do not expect to see everything plain here: 'For now we see through a glass darkly, but then face to face; now I know in part, but then shall I know even as also I am known.'

So it is the pursuit of truth that is our duty; in Langland's poem the search for truth is presented as a great pilgrimage, or a series of pilgrimages, and the poem ends almost as it begins with Conscience setting out on a new journey:

> 'By Christ,' said Conscience then, 'I will become a pilgrim and walk as wide as the world lasts.'

My vision of education − and I am sure all at Keble share it − is of a common pilgrimage (of teachers and taught alike) to what Langland fancifully describes as the shrine of Saint Truth.

When all treasures are tried, truth is the best.

In that search for truth, I hope we shall recognize that the truth of experience − the true life − is as much to be sought for as the truth of books or the laboratory bench − and that we shall ever use as touchstones in our search the tests of quality and value. Do what you will, but do it well! Whether it is a weekly essay, or a football match, or an address in chapel, let us strive for excellence and be satisfied with nothing less than the best we can do. The quality of achievement is one test; the other is value. Ask yourselves all the time whether what you are devoting your life to is valuable − or sufficiently valuable − or more valuable than the alternatives. And in assessing value the critical questions are: how does this activity serve others? ('Inasmuch as ye have done it unto one of the least of these my brethren, ye have done it unto me'); how does this activity fulfil and perfect yourself? ('Be ye perfect, even as your Father in heaven is perfect'); is it fun? − You will be wondering where in the New Testament I will draw scriptural support for the view that life and thought are intended to be, ought to be fun. Christ's biographers were, I think, solemn men though I doubt whether he was: but listen to John Donne writing about the wit of God:

> My *God*, my *God*, Thou art a *direct God*, may I not say a *literall God*, a *God* that wouldest bee understood *literally*, and according to the *plaine* sense of all that thou saiest? But thou art also (*Lord*, I intend it to thy *glory*, and let no *prophane misinterpreter* abuse it to thy *diminution*), thou art a *figurative*, a *metaphoricall God too*: a *God* in whose words there is such a height of *figures*, such *voyages*, such *peregrinations* to fetch remote and precious *metaphors*, such *extensions*, such *spreadings*, such *Curtaines* of *Allegories*, such *third Heavens*, of *Hyperboles, so harmonious eloqutions*, so *retired* and so *reserved expressions*, so *commanding perswasions*, so *perswading commandements*, such *sinewes* even in thy *milke* and such *things* in thy *words*, as all *prophane Authors*, seeme of the seed of the *Serpent*, that *creepes*, thou art the *Dove*, that flies.

I think Langland would have understood Donne's celebration of God's wit: he certainly recognized the sheer fun of life in his account of the pilgrimage to truth. As the pilgrims are about to set out, Piers Plowman himself first enters the poem and describes the difficult route they have to follow – so difficult is it that the pilgrims are discouraged from even starting and are soon distracted by other things. As someone says: 'this were a wicked way, unless one had a guide'.

The pursuit of Truth is indeed a rough and arduous pilgrimage, and we need the best guides available. Piers Powman gives a hint, echoing the instruction of 'Kynde' (or Nature) who had advised Will on the crafts he should study:

> Learn to love, and leave all other.

Piers' account of the pilgrimage to truth, after describing a long, complicated and dangerous journey, finishes like this:

> And if Grace grant thee to go in this wise
> Thou shalt see in thyself Truth sit in thy heart
> In a chain of charity.

2

The Problem of English

Few will now remember the row which blew up in the Cambridge English Faculty in early 1981, nor should they. The editor of *The Times Literary Supplement* took the opportunity of inviting a number of people to contribute to a symposium on the nature of English studies. For me this proved a chance (or a challenge) to write about my subject. I have always considered myself a professional student of the English language, and an amateur of literature. It is relatively easy to explain why — and how — one should study language (though some make heavy weather of it), but the study of literature seems to me almost insuperably difficult. The concerns expressed in this essay have stayed in my mind — the issue of creativity is picked up again in Chapter 5, for example, the question of evaluation is addressed most directly in Chapter 20. (I was finally convinced of the cultural importance of the medium of television — by the arguments of our children — a year or so after suggesting it here, when we bought our first TV.) When this was written, English studies, and the humanities generally, were flourishing. Today the appropiate role and extent of the humanities in higher education is very much in question, the issues of creativity, of evaluation and of popular culture are more than ever important.

It would be impertinent for me to comment on the details of the remarkable row which has suddenly erupted in the Cambridge English Faculty, because it is difficult at a distance to disentangle the personal issues, the ideological questions and the sheer struggle for power.

I write from Oxford: there, one feels, but for the grace of Gardner go we. It may not be improper, though, to consider some of the broader issues raised by the Cambridge crisis. Why is it English (or literary studies, at least) that generates these fierce theoretical conflicts these days? Is it possible, or desirable, to determine the right way to study English? What is the real crisis in English studies?

In the Middle Ages it was theology ('queen of sciences') which was thought to hold the secrets of the universe. Theology gave place to philosophy, and other subjects have flourished briefly and disappointed our unreasonable expectations. Was sociology going to save the world or linguistics reveal the structure of the human brain? For some time now, astonishingly, English has been fashionable and has seemed to offer answers to the old unanswerable questions.

Although in times of economic decline and recession students understandably turn towards 'vocational' subjects — medicine, veterinary science, law, for example — the unrelenting pressure for places on English courses contradicts this trend and poses a problem. What do all these able students flocking to the English departments of universities and polytechnics and colleges of higher education hope to find? And can we satisfy them?

The days are gone when gentlemen merely cultivated a personal taste and called it reading English. English studies today are real and earnest, and students rightly demand serious answers — which means answers with a theoretical framework — to serious questions. Unfortunately, literature is strongly resistant to theory — or, rather, it accommodates all theories while failing to provide an adequate test for them. Untestable theories cannot be proved wrong, but they cannot be shown to be right, either. And the frustration that is created in English studies by the unresolved jostling of Marxism, structuralism, post-structuralism and the rest with the many variants of traditional 'Eng. Lit.', conceals a deeper anxiety: that possibly the subject is not really an academic discipline at all.

At the heart of English studies lie, uneasily twisted together, two basic questions. The first is: why is this work the way it is? The answer may be: because the literary tradition from which it sprang was so; or, because the author was the person he or she was; or, because the society which engendered it was of a certain nature; or because the language of the time was thus and not otherwise; and so on. While the order of importance is debatable, it would not be unreasonable to think that each of these answers is likely to be partly true. Academic hyperbole, however, all too often invites us to pretend that one approach is entirely successful, and the rest are rubbish. The second question is: why, and how, is this work valuable? It is tempting to sidestep this subjective and difficult matter and concentrate instead on the apparently more scientific study of the nature of literature. But, apart from the fact that the latter question is for many the more urgent and important of the two, it is not possible to devote one's life (or a large part of it) to the former without first — albeit provisionally or implicitly — facing the question of value, or begging it.

Serious as these questions are, however, they do not strike me as the most critical ones facing English studies at present — perhaps because they are always with us. I have sometimes thought that the critical issue for English studies was the challenge of creative writing: why it is that, for all our vaunted expertise, we shy away from teaching the practice of fictional prose or verse or drama, or (if we do it at all) do it with no obvious success? The medieval rhetoricians were not so timid. The few courses in Britain that tackle this issue (such as the one at the Sheffield Polytechnic) merit our respect. But the real issue is a different one. While higher education in this field concerns itself almost exclusively with traditional literary 'high culture', the community at large has turned for its most influential form of cultural expression and experience to television. The general public, our students — and many of the teachers — prefer *Dallas* to *Daniel Deronda*. It was not expected, when our society embarked on the great educational adventure of the last hundred years, that this would be the result, and we have yet to come to terms with it.

What is to be done? I would be suspicious of dramatic or extreme solutions to the problems of English studies. One of the great strengths of how the subject is taught in higher education in Britain is the extraordinary variety and liberal choice of courses available to students. That is as it should be. In designing, or redesigning, English courses, we should be seeking the best possible equation between the aims of the particular course (which implies that it should have explicit and defensible aims), the available 'resources' (above all, the teachers on hand — rather than the ones we hanker after but cannot have) and the syllabuses. And we should probably admit that it is of the nature of the subject that any course will be, at best, no more than a brave and interesting failure. All English dons tend to think that changing the course will solve all problems; all students believe that altering the examination arrangements will bring about the millennium. They are both wrong: it is teaching that matters. Good teachers not only know their subject but set themselves clear and definite objectives and work out methods of evaluating their own success. English is an exhilarating subject. Our task is to make it rigorous, without losing the exhilaration. Outbursts of passionate concern — for such is the crisis at Cambridge — are a sign of life. And when English as a subject no longer produces students and teachers who fiercely question the whole basis of the subject, it will die.

3

The Advancement of Education

The traditional universities are chartered institutions. Their charters empower them to offer courses and award degrees, without the need for external approval or validation. In the 'public sector', on the other hand, among the polytechnics and colleges of higher education, no diploma or degree course may be offered without the approval of the Secretary of State and validation by a university, the Business and Technician Education Council (BTEC) or the Council for National Academic Awards (CNAA). This lecture, which was given at Thames Polytechnic in June 1981, drew on fourteen years of experience as a member of CNAA and tried to assess the value of the Council's work. In particular, it confronted squarely the question of whether one could reconcile a firm belief in the value of external validation for the public sector with the widespread prejudice in universities that external validation could be of no use to them. I have not changed my views. And in 1985, with the report of the Lindop Committee on the CNAA expected shortly, these issues are once again in question.

'Upon the education of the people of this country the fate of this country depends.' This is as true today as it was in 1874 when in the House of Commons it was spoken by Disraeli. (I should like to hear a Conservative Prime Minister — any Prime Minister, for that matter — say it with conviction in the Commons today!) It is a strange time to be talking of 'the advancement of education': in the present economic climate, with the present government's policies on public expenditure — especially with regard to higher education — one might be forgiven for speaking of a decline: like Matthew Arnold, thinking of the sea of faith on Dover beach, we 'only hear/Its melancholy long withdrawing roar/Retreating....' And yet, it is a peculiar and endearing feature of the educational history of this country that some of the boldest advances have been made at the bleakest times of national crisis. One thinks of King Alfred's imaginative letter to his bishops, the first Royal Commission on Education, establishing the first state school in England in the year 891 or thereabouts, when the country was partly overrun by Danish invaders; or the foundation of a number of Oxford colleges in the darkest periods of the fifteenth century, or indeed the planning and enactment of the great Butler Education Act of 1944 during the Second World War. And so, in the present national crisis — which rather pales into insignificance beside these earlier periods of real emergency — I do not think it inappropriate to be talking of 'the advancement of education, learning, knowledge and the arts'.

My title is a quotation: drawn from paragraph two of the Charter of the Council for National Academic Awards (CNAA). The full text is as follows:

> The object of the Council shall be the advancement in our United Kingdom of Great Britain and Northern Ireland of education, learning, knowledge and the arts by means of the grant of academic awards and distinctions; and for the purpose of promoting that object it shall, subject to the provisions of this Our Charter and of the Statutes of the Council, determine the conditions governing the grant of such awards and distinctions and approve courses of study to be pursued by candidates to qualify for such grants, including where appropriate, arrangements for training and experience in industry or commerce associated with such courses.

My purpose is to ask how, and how far, the Council has achieved its objective of 'the advancement of education, learning, knowledge and the arts'. Any attempt to answer such a question must (at this stage, and by a single witness) be tentative, partial, idiosyncratic and entirely unofficial. If it stimulates others to provide better and fuller assessments, it will not have been altogether valueless.

Exactly twenty years ago saw the setting up of the Committee on Higher Education chaired by Lord Robbins which, when it reported in 1963, recommended the establishment of the CNAA, in place of the National Council for Technological Awards; it was to be set up under Royal Charter, to extend its influence over the whole of Great Britain, to cover areas of study, not only within, but also outside, science and technology, and to draw its membership from industry, from what we now call the public sector institutions, and from the universities. All this has duly come about. Indeed it had come about as early as 1967 when I was first invited to join the CNAA as a member of the newly-established English Studies Board. It is still not clear to me why the members of the CNAA are prepared to work for it: the question is particularly pertinent in the case of university members. Is it the seriousness and importance of the task? Or a reprehensible lust for power? Or the quality of the dinners? Or the value of the friendships one makes? Or the opportunity to escape from time to time from the problems of one's own institution? In my own case, although I would not deny that each of these motives applies to some extent, what initially drew me to the CNAA was the realization that the Council's degrees were gradually and inevitably replacing the external degree system of the University of London. I had grown up believing that London's external system was Britain's greatest contribution to higher education: an exaggerated belief, perhaps, but remember that my father was then the external registrar of the University of London!

London had provided for two needs: the needs of the individual (often part-time) student, and the needs of a large number of developing institutions which required access to the opportunity of teaching at the higher education level. While the London external system has not completely disappeared, it remains broadly true that the first need is now mainly provided for by the Open University, while the CNAA attempts to satisfy the second. Those who have had experience of teaching for a London external degree will not need reminding of the disadvantages of that system, at least for the teacher: the inflexibility of courses and syllabuses, which did not (indeed could not) respond to the interests and capabilities of those who taught them; and the brutality of a validation process which effectively controlled the standard only of the final examination. It was a system which inevitably produced alarming student wastage, and frustrated the teachers. But there can be no doubt that it was a simple and effective method of ensuring that London external degrees were (I quote from the 8th Statute of the CNAA) 'comparable in standards to awards granted and conferred by universities'. It is to be questioned whether the Council's system of validation, in spite of its many and very real merits, can yet provide the guarantee of quality that the old London external degree offered.

When one reads over the Charter and Statutes of the Council today − the current version is in fact dated March 1974 − it is clear that, as one would expect, there have been a number of developments within the Council which were not exactly envisaged when they were written. I should like to consider two in particular: the development − and growing importance − of the system of 'institutional validation'; and the growth in number, importance and strength of the subject boards.

Although I am now a member of the Council's Committee for Institutions, and have frequently taken part in quinquennial review visits, and officers' visits, and what are now renamed institutional review visits, I must confess to an ineradicable scepticism about the appropriateness and value of this part of the Council's work. First of all, we may note that it is extremely difficult to find in the Charter and Statutes a justification for the notion (and practice) of approving *institutions* (as opposed to *courses*). The Council certainly has the power to set up committees to approve courses... and (I quote) *'perform such other functions as the Council may from time to time require'*: and the functions of the committees include 'approval of courses of study... having had regard to the standard of work in the subject of a course at the establishment at which it is being pursued *and the facilities available thereat for that course'*. But these are slender constitutional threads upon which to hang the whole paraphernalia of institutional validation.

Be that as it may, there are more serious and more down-to-earth objections to the system of institutional reviews. In brief, it is *impractical, unreal, impertinent* and *unprofessional. Impractical* − because a committee which meets a bare half dozen times a year cannot take effective responsibility for evaluating the institutional health of more than 150 colleges and polytechnics. Visiting parties on institutional review visits rarely contain more than two or three members of the committee responsible for ordering the visit, and never have an opportunity to discuss the visit papers in the office before deciding whether a visit would be appropriate − as is normal practice in the subject boards. The sheer weight of work makes such a system (desirable though it might be) administratively impractical. *Unreal* − because the idea of giving (or not giving) approval to an institution is based on a bad analogy with *course-approval*. It is possible − it often happens − for a subject board to reject a new course proposal; it is also possible − it happens rarely — for a subject board to refuse to renew an existing course, though the political difficulties of such a decision are substantial. But I doubt whether it is really possible to refuse to approve an institution — except in the special circumstances of an institution new to the Council's work and without any approved courses. *Impertinent* — because it has seemed to me either arrogant or absurd for a group of people, however carefully selected or well-intentioned, to descend on a complex institution and expect after one short day's work to arrive at a satisfactory verdict on the whole institution. With a very few exceptions, however, the colleges and polytechnics seem curiously content to suffer these visitations and to respond to the eventual reports, without complaint. *Unprofessional* — because no one can be an expert on institutions: again, the analogy wih subject-board visits is unhelpful. Institutional review visits are necessarily conducted by amateurs, and run the inevitable risk of seeming to be merely amateurish.

The question I ask is whether institutional reviews will (can) ever be a fully satisfactory part of the Council's work. One would not feel so concerned to ask the question were it not that the Council is, with the establishment of a special Committee for Institutions, giving added emphasis and authority to its work at institutional level. I should prefer to see a development towards the idea of unlimited institutional approval, after the initial successful visit, with the retention of the institutional review visit for three limited purposes: (i) for the initial vetting of colleges new to the Council's work; (ii) as an advisory service available to any of the Council's colleges and polytechnics that would like a thorough external review of some (or all) aspects of the institution; (iii) as an option available to the Council, in the event of seriously adverse reports from subject-board visiting parties, to enable the CNAA to intervene in, and review, an unsatisfactory institutional situation. Although one would hope that it would be a rare occurrence, in the real and all too fallible world one must make provision for the possibility of organizational failure, planning disaster, managerial incompetence, a crippling reduction in funding, and so on. In such situations, I should want the Council to retain the option of intervening decisively at institutional level.

The Charter and Statutes are absolutely clear that the way in which the Council is to achieve its objects is by the *approval of courses* through the work of the subject committees and their related and subordinate subject boards. With some exceptions, the subject committees have never really fulfilled the role that was expected of them. My own experience is limited to the Committee for Arts and Social Studies of which I have been a member since 1973, but I do not believe that this experience has been untypical. Over the years the Committees have, not inappropriately — and entirely in accordance with section 4 subsection (3) of the Charter — delegated their *de facto* powers to their boards and reserved to themselves the more limited role of reviewing general policy questions and exercising (at most) a somewhat loose and informal control over the activities of the boards. This is not surprising: the committees do not meet very often and they are not always well-attended when they do meet. The effectiveness of any Committee in any walk of life depends not a little on the amount of work its members are prepared to do. The subject boards work hard. It is the main thesis of this lecture that if the Council has in its short life made any contribution to 'the advancement of education, learning, knowledge and the arts' it is primarily through the work of the subject boards. I say 'if' because a central feature of the work of the subject boards is that they do not direct or lead or prescribe, but act responsively to facilitate the realization of courses conceived and designed in the institutions. It is, of course, the institutions which directly achieve 'the advancement of education, learning, knowledge and the arts'.

The 'responsive' nature of the subject boards' work needs a little more consideration, not only because it is (in my view) so essential a feature of what the Council has achieved, but also because it is an attitude and an approach that is extraordinarily difficult for academics to maintain: 'Here is a task for all that a man has of fortitude and delicacy' (R.L. Stevenson was speaking of family life, but it will serve in the present context). We academics love to teach, and our instruction all too easily turns into dictation. The temptation to take a hand at course design must be almost irresistible for the members of most subject boards: but it must always be strenuously resisted — and it usually is. Contrast, if you will, this flexibility, responsiveness, and — as far as is humanly possible — absence of preconception, which are characteristic of the best work of the subject boards with the necessarily more rigid statements of policy within which both the boards and the course planning teams must operate. I am thinking, above all, of the *Regulations* which lay down detailed rules and guidelines on such subjects as admissions requirements, length of course, examination arrangements, and so on. It is one of the functions of the higher level bodies — the committees and specialist working parties — to produce these official policy statements, guidelines or regulations, call them what you will. It is the function of the subject boards to co-operate with the course planning teams in the institutions to provide flexible and acceptable interpretations of the rules. One example, what used to be called Clause 4 and is now Principle 3, demands that the Council's courses should make a serious attempt to provide educative range and contrast, that (for instance) science courses should find room for some literary and humane study, and arts courses should include some provision for work requiring numeracy or the methods of the exact sciences. Not all course teams have been willing to observe Principle 3, and subject boards have had a difficult task deciding how far they should insist on the strict observance of the rule. The task was not made any easier by the fact that some arts boards, and many members (especially university members of the CNAA) have little sympathy themselves with Principle 3. The upshot is that, although on the science side the rule is observed pretty rigorously (I understand), in the humanities it is probably honoured more in the breach than the observance. I make no comment on whether this is a good or bad state of affairs, but use the example to underline my claim that a central feature of the subject boards' approach to their work has been a remarkably flexible responsiveness to the course designs submitted by the institutions, even to the extent of bending the Council's own rules.

The result has been to allow an astonishing range of pioneering courses exploring new ground in syllabus content (eg leisure activities or the performing arts), in course design (eg modular degrees, integrated and unintegrated combined studies degrees ranging across the faculties), in examination arrangements, and in many other aspects.

If *responsiveness* is the first characteristic of the subject boards' work which springs to mind, the second is equally important: it is the principle of *validation by peers*, the idea that it is appropriate for a course planning team's work to be judged by a group of fellow-professionals, teachers and scholars in the same subject. Perhaps this idea now seems so obvious that you will not consider it worth dwelling on; however, we may note that the universities have not yet hit upon it, or adopted it from the public sector – and in my view they are the poorer thereby. The principle of validation by peers lies at the heart of the Council's claims to be doing a professional job, and it is the basis on which any degree of confidence in the CNAA must be built. At its best, the principle requires that the members of subject boards and visiting parties should be scholars and teachers of outstanding professional reputation who command the ungrudging respect of their peers in higher education. In the real world such men and women are hard to find, and (if they are found) there are many calls upon their time. When you recall that the Council has to balance subject-board membership between the public and private sectors of higher education, and (where appropriate) industrial and other outside members, and to ensure continuity without stagnation by rolling reviews of membership and regulated changes; when you remember the need to ensure appropriate cross-membership between related boards (linguistics, for example, must have intersecting membership with English studies, languages, combined studies, philosophy, and communication studies), and note the importance of providing an experienced chairman (and training the next chairman); when you bear in mind all these interlocking requirements, I think you will agree that the Council does not do too badly in selecting its members. But it is of the utmost importance that the quality of the membership is maintained. The institutions, which nominate through academic boards many names for consideration, must avoid the temptation of thinking that membership of a subject board is an appropriate reward for long service and good conduct, or that it is the right of every course leader to sit on the relevant subject board, or even that the purpose of nominating a colleague for one of the Council's boards is primarily to provide a channel of information and expertise to flow from Grays Inn Road into the institution. The only good reason for nominating a colleague for consideration as a member of a subject board is the conviction that as an outstanding scholar and teacher he or she will make a substantial contribution to the Council's work.

Responsiveness not prescription: validation by peers. The third feature I want to draw your attention to is the requirement the subject boards make of an *explicit statement* of the course proposal. They can do little else; if they are to take the responsibility of approving a course, they must know what it is that they are approving. But the value to the course team – and to the course itself – of requiring an explicit, defensible, written statement of the course is enormous. I have often heard course leaders admit that the requirement the Council makes of them to state – and often restate – the substance of a course has led to substantial and unexpected improvements. And we can often see this happening when a course has to be submitted two or three times before it is finally approved. All schemes can be improved, of course, by revision: and revision can be endless. One of the disciplines a subject board must impose upon itself is not to require an intolerable series of resubmissions of a broadly acceptable course merely in the hope of stimulating marginal improvements. It is a difficult question of judgement and experience to know when enough is enough: I don't suppose we always get it right! But I would draw your attention to the contrast between the requirement for *explicit statement* in the work of the CNAA with the marked absence of any such discipline in the university sector. One of the central weaknesses of much university course design is the failure to make, and confront, an explicit statement of the proposal.

A good course design is like a tripod; it should be firmly balanced on three legs. Most of the rejections issued by subject boards arise from a failure to match and reconcile the *aims of a submission*, with *the available resources* (including, and especially, the teaching team), and *the design of the course*. (The other main cause of failure for CNAA submissions is the delicate issue of an adverse judgement on the quality of the course team.) If only those who design courses or those responsible for internal validation, would insist rigorously on this essential reconciliation of *objectives, resources* and *course*, much of a subject board's work would be done for it.

I have tried to argue that the central features of the work of the subject boards can be summed up in the following phrases: (i) responsiveness rather than prescription; (ii) validation by peers; (iii) the requirement of explicit statement; (iv) the reconciliation of objectives, resources and the course. At the end of the day the subject board is, however, faced with the difficult question of standards. For the boards are responsible, through their committees, to the Council for 'ensuring that the awards granted by the Council are comparable in standard to awards granted and conferred by universities'. Judgement of standards in higher education is rarely as scientific or objective as we would wish: and subject boards are given little advice or help in their thankless task of drawing a line between the acceptable and the unacceptable course proposal. The *Robbins Report* is at its weakest when it talks of standards: 'we must demand of a system that it produces as much high excellence as possible. It must therefore be so devised that it safeguards standards.' Ah, but how? and how are they to be measured? As I recall, it was normal in the early days of the Council to refer quite explicitly (if anecdotally) to the standards of particular university courses when a board was considering a submission from a course team. This threw a particular responsibility on the university members of boards, who consequently played a greater role in validation than the other members. That, I am glad to say, is not the practice today: instead we are all content to refer to the Council's own standards as the essential yardstick – though the question of their definition and measurement is as difficult as ever. – One other point on the subject of standards: I note that boards often ask themselves two different (and not necessarily compatible) questions about the standards of a proposed course. The first is: whether the course achieves the Council's minimum acceptable standard? The second is: whether it represents the best course the staff are capable of designing and teaching? What is a board to do when the answer to the first question is 'Yes', and to the second 'No'? If the object of the exercise is the advancement of education, learning, knowledge and the arts, presumably the board should ask for a resubmission... or should it?

I said earlier that I was sceptical of the value of the practice of *institutional validation*. I cannot have left you in any doubt that I set enormous value on the system of *course approval* through the subject boards. It is my thesis that it is here that the Council has made its major contribution to British higher education. When a university member of the CNAA speaks in such words he invites a telling response: 'If you think the system of course approval is so valuable in public sector institutions, why do you not argue for its extension to the universities?' Well, I am prepared to accept the challenge and state that I believe it should be so extended. It could not do university courses anything but good to be reviewed by the CNAA in the same way, and with the same rigour, as is currently applied to courses in public sector institutions. It could not do the Council anything but good to be able to make a direct assessment of the comparability of standards between its own awards and those of the universities, just as its statutes require. Is this practical politics, you will wonder? ... I don't know, but I should like to see the Council exploring the possibility of offering, initially on an advisory and informal basis, and for the sake of the education of its own boards, a service to the universities of objective course validation to supplement the universities' own internal methods. I dream of a day when the government will reintegrate the two parts of our extraordinary binary system of higher education, and when (and if) that happens, hope that rather than allowing the Council to wither away the government will consider the extension of the full CNAA system of course validation to all institutions including the most ancient of the universities. (If university courses are as good as we think they are, we should have nothing to fear: if they are not, the sooner we know, and improve them, the better.)

Believing as I do in the value of the subject boards I deplore any attempt to reduce their effectiveness or role. The recent development in the Council's work known as 'partnership in validation' has been seen by some as a limitation of the powers and responsibilities of the boards, while providing for an extension of the role of the Committee for Institutions within the Council, and an invitation to the institutions themselves to play a fuller part in the validation process. I do not see it like that. Unfortunately, partnership in validation has come to mean all things to all men. If the new system of partnership encourages the institutions to take a greater responsibility for maintaining the standards of their courses, it will be wholly to the good. But nothing can deprive the committees of the Council and their dependent subject boards of the responsibility of providing the ultimate definition of the acceptable standards for the Council's work, and ensuring and facilitating the 'advancement of education, learning, knowledge and the arts'.

I am concerned about the CNAA for two more reasons. First, it is a remarkably shy organization, rarely seeking publicity, and making little attempt to educate the general public about its work and its achievement. I have long regretted this, and now feel that such excessive modesty is a positive fault. The quantity, range, and quality of the higher education provided under the umbrella of the CNAA in the public sector is not nearly as well and widely known as it should be. The Council's own procedures, the members it has attracted − the quality and spirit of its officers, the weight of work that is dispatched in a year − all these things should be brought more to the attention of the public, and made more of. Those of us who have served the Council during the last decade and a half have witnessed the making of a little bit of history in British education: the story is worth telling and should not be left unwritten. I should like to see the Council pay much more attention to publicizing and reporting its own achievements and those of public sector higher education in general.

Secondly, *quis custodiet ipsos custodes?* It is a strange thing that the Council, so ready to pass judgement on the work of others, so insistent (these days) on the need for rigorous procedures of internal validation, has never — as far as I know — given thought to the question of the validation of its own activities. At the very least, one might expect the Council to have developed its own processes of internal validation, the monitoring of the work of the boards by their parent committees or by *ad hoc* groups of members and officers. It could be argued that this sort of thing goes on all the time in an informal sort of way. But when one of the Council's institutions says something like that about its procedures for internal validation, we are not satisfied — and rightly so. The CNAA ought to turn its mind to the question of its own validation, first by developing explicit and known procedures for internal validation, and secondly by considering the possibiliy of inviting external validation, perhaps by a group of experienced past chairmen and ex-members. The new appeal procedure is not nearly enough to meet this need. Here is an area where the institutions in the public sector could with justification provide constructive criticism of the CNAA and help to ensure that what is (in my view) already a remarkably successful and original enterprise continues to function and perform as effectively as is humanly possible.

I began with Disraeli's words on the importance of education, and I make no apology for returning to them. 'Upon the education of the people of this country the fate of this country depends'. In the present climate of opinion, with concern to cut back public expenditure, it is unfashionable, and will seem like special pleading to make high claims for the importance of our systems of higher education. But we should not be afraid to do so. And the claim for higher education should not be based on our understandable desire to preserve jobs, or protect vested interests, or avoid the agonies of change. It should be based upon a common recognition of the importance of promoting the 'advancement of education, learning, knowledge and the arts'. Twenty years ago the Robbins Committee set to work on a planned development of higher education until 1980. We are now one year into the era for which there is no adequate or agreed plan. I note with interest the proposal for an SRHE Leverhulme inquiry into higher education. I hope this will prove not to be just a 'voice crying in the wilderness', but may turn out to be a forerunner of the Royal Commission which we now so badly need. The next public inquiry into higher education will have many tasks, but central among them I suggest will be the redefinition and clarification of the *objectives of higher education*; the reassessment of the *acceptable standards of higher education*; the design of an effective system of *organization and control of higher education*. Such a system must solve the problem of the appropriate balance between national and local planning, and the legitimate and necessary freedom of institutions to develop in their own ways, and it must distinguish and make appropriate arrangements for each of the three strands in the control of higher education — funding, planning, and validation. And in that system I believe the CNAA has a vital role to play.

4
Hard Times in Higher Education

The Trent Polytechnic graduation ceremony of November 1981 was the first of a number of such occasions for me as speaker, of which the most recent was at The Hatfield Polytechnic (see Chapter 20). I hope that any graduate, or diplomate, who reads this — from among the many I have addressed in the intervening three years — will forgive me when he or she discovers that the speech was adapted (rather than completely rewritten) for each successive occasion. The main themes — and they also recur again and again in this volume — are the need for clearly defined educational objectives and the desirability of the gradual integration of our two systems of higher education (the traditional universities, and the polytechnics and colleges in the public sector). When I spoke at Trent, I had no idea that within a month I was to become Chairman of the Board of the 'interim National Body' (now the National Advisory Body for Public Sector Higher Education, or NAB), and therefore directly responsible — with others — for tackling these and similar issues in the planning of higher education.

These are indeed hard times in higher education, and in education generally. We face some difficult problems; and I do not so much think of the inadequacy of our resources or the financial constraints — real though these are. Nor do I refer to the sad fact that (whatever you think of this government's desire to control and reduce public expenditure in higher education) the reduction is being done too fast, too thoughtlessly, and (unless at the very least, it is phased in over a reasonable period of time — say five or six years) it will result in unnecessary further damage and waste in a system of education that has served, and is serving, the country honourably and well. No: that is not my theme today. I am thinking rather of the confusion and uncertainty of our objectives, the feeling (widespread today) that education — especially higher education — has somehow lost its way.

During this last century we have seen astonishing and far-reaching developments in education in Britain, producing the school-system of today, the many universities, and a wide range of colleges and institutions of further education, out of which grew the polytechnics. And this great advancement of education and learning, which we now so readily take for granted, has been accompanied by a dramatic rise in the expectation of what could be achieved by means of more and better education. In brief, we thought – and hoped and believed – that it would make our society richer, juster, and better. But it doesn't seem to have done so.

My own conviction is that we are misguided if we make wealth, or social justice, or moral improvement the *direct aim* of our education, or if we think that these desirable qualities will be the *inevitable result* of turning people into graduates. But they are very often the *indirect* consequence or the corollary of education, and I firmly believe that our society is (at least) a *little* richer, juster and better now than it would have been if we had not embarked on the great educational adventure of the last 100 years!

So we must not lose heart (though some who should know better are doing so). We should not lose heart in higher education if the gross national product shows a temporary fall, or if the truly equal society seems still a distant dream, or if graduates and lecturers seem no better than other men and women: those things – though desirable – were never what higher education was for. And if new graduates are finding that the right job – or any job – is not easily come by, that the society they are entering is not (yet) firmly based on the principle of equality of opportunity – whether we look at the plight of the inner cities, or of Northern Ireland, or even at the educational system itself – they too should not lose heart, or fall into the twin traps of indolence or despair.

As a nation we tend to expect too much of the latest fashionable enterprise – be it 'the white heat of technology', or the Robbins principle, or monetarism, or the microchip – to expect too much and then complain piteously when our new fad, our new god, lets us down.

The real crisis in higher education will come, I suggest, if we let ourselves be sidetracked from our proper purpose to follow secondary aims, which we cannot realize. What is our proper purpose? Nothing more – or less – than the *pursuit of truth*.

The pursuit of truth is no easy task, nor is it a soft option. Those who have just graduated, and who have wrestled with the question for three years, know that, as John Donne tells us:

> On a huge hill,
> Cragged and steep, Truth stands and he that will
> Reach her, about must and about must go,
> And what the hill's suddenness resists, win so.

What we all have in common in higher education is the common pursuit of truth as our first principle: the second is the very British idea that scholarship and learning, though in essence solitary activities, are best carried forward in communities, in colleges and polytechnics and universities where social life may flourish among the libraries and laboratories and lecture halls. And building such communities and making them effective societies is not easy: we must never forget the need to communicate freely with each of the several parts of our academic societies, to avoid alienation, and to promote mutual understanding.

Abraham Cowley prayed for 'a few friends and many books, both true'.

And, though I suspect that some of my students have wished rather for 'many friends and a few books', nevertheless I like Cowley's idea of education. Polytechnics and universities share these ideals of the pursuit of truth, and the fostering of the scholarly community. And the more I see of both sectors of higher education, the more I am struck by what they have in common. They agree on principles, and differ in detail. *Vive la différence*! But, as in the case of the two sexes, let us not forget that we need one another, and belong to a single species. We can learn much from the other's behaviour − I am thinking of universities and polytechnics now, not the sexes! − and one lesson that the universities must begin to learn from the polytechnics is the recognition of an obligation to the local community, and of the value of firm roots in, and links with, local industry, commerce and public service. Another is the enormous value of the external validation of courses. Whether the polytechnics could learn useful lessons from the universities it is not for me to say, though I should hope they might. Our universities and polytechnics (our so-called private and public sectors of higher education) have at heart much more in common than their superficial differences would suggest, and must come closer together. It is high time that the binary system disappeared, and that the universities were admitted into the public sector.

I welcome the establishment of the interim National Body for funding the polytechnics and the colleges − *provided* that it recognizes that one of its first duties and tasks must be to make contact with, and work with, the University Grants Committee.

I would also welcome any move to bring closer together our staff associations and unions in the twin sectors of higher education. Here, the students have set us an excellent example: it is high time we followed it.

5

The Best Modern Way

The Leverhulme programme of study into the future of higher education (see Chapter 11) was the series of nine broadly-based residential seminars held by the Society for Research into Higher Education between 1981 and 1983, of which the fifth, funded by the Gulbenkian Foundation and concerned with the arts, was held at Keble in the spring of 1982. I was invited to chair the seminar. I remember a formless but exhilarating debate, as we attempted to work out a rationale for the arts in higher education. This essay, which provided a foreword for the book of the seminar (Robinson 1982), is concerned with the related questions of the role of the arts in society and in education. The range and balance of the curriculum in higher education is a perennial problem. What should we teach? And why?

'I walk through the long schoolroom questioning....' W.B. Yeats's great poem *Among Schoolchildren* provided an apt point of departure for a discussion of the role of the arts in education – more specifically, for a seminar devoted to the arts in higher education. The series of nine SRHE Leverhulme seminars have ranged through 'the long schoolroom' which stretches from the primary school to the PhD – from the oldest universities to the newest polytechnics and colleges – 'from China to Peru' – from the sciences to the humanities – the practical to the theoretical – from Plato's Academy ('a corporate body organized for the worship of the muses') or the medieval educational system of the seven liberal arts (including music and rhetoric) to Keble's and Newman's Oxford or the more recent flowering of higher education following the Robbins Report.

> ... learn to cipher and to sing,
> To study reading-books and histories,
> To cut and sew, be neat in everything
> In the best modern way. ...

Our task is to redefine 'the best modern way' in higher education.

Academic debate these days all too often tends to confront means rather than ends, and to concern itself with immediate problems rather than review the experience of the past or plan for a better future. But before we discuss details of course design, or the provision of funds for the arts, or the problems of assessment, we must face squarely the question of value. Why should the arts have a place in higher education? What role should they play?

The answer to these questions depends not a little on the answer to a prior question: what is the value, or role, of the arts in our society? And here we must confront the views of those on the one hand who think that the arts are like excess baggage which travellers sensibly jettison when the going gets rough, and those on the other side who, finding the question 'why the arts?' similar to (and quite as unanswerable as) 'why live?', believe that the arts constitute part of the irreducible core and essence of our civilization and culture. But do they? It is quite easy (though wrong) to conclude that the arts are an optional extra in our daily lives of getting and spending. If our idea of life is confined to the material and consumable goods, the arts (like love) seem dispensable. And the argument that the arts themselves form an important industry – though undeniable – is not itself the foundation of the case for the arts. Not all values are reducible to economic terms. 'Man shall not live by bread alone.'

In the ordinary round of social life, whether in the family, the college, or the nation, we recognize four compelling aspirations (or ambitions, or appetites) for which men and women will sometimes set aside the normal rules of conduct, when tempted. They are wealth, power, art and love. The Gospels tell how Jesus was tempted with the offer of wealth and power; and literature and legend remind us of such figures as Mammon and Macbeth, Marsyas and Mark Antony. It is not difficult to think of other examples – in legend, literature or life – where the world has seemed well lost in the face of the overwhelming temptations of wealth or power – or art or love ('... they too break hearts.'). I suppose each of these forceful impulses to be morally neutral in themselves: it is the business of living to channel them towards good ends.

In earlier times man has attempted to define God in just these terms: possessing all things, omnipotent, creative, all-loving. The first three chapters of *Genesis* elaborate the idea of God sharing his attributes (all save immortality) with mankind. 'God created man in his own image.' The yearnings to possess, to control, to create, and to adore, represent the deepest aspirations of man, and constitute the heart of what we understand as human life, and imagine of the divinity. The case for the arts rests, in my view, on the belief that creativity ('man the maker') is inherent and essential in humanity.

I realize that those already convinced of the value of the arts will find this argument a lame and feeble attempt to prove the obvious; and that those who are not so convinced will continue, like the Philistines, to persecute Samson. But perhaps even they may pause and reflect, if they consider the extraordinarily high value our society (rightly) places on the surviving arts of our predecessors, and the devotion and expense lavished upon our libraries and museums and galleries, upon concert-halls and theatres and cinemas. While two views might be taken of the question whether enough public money is spent in this way, no one can doubt that it is a striking characteristic of our society (and of others) to treasure, and try to preserve, the surviving arts – the pyramids or the *Oresteia*. The arts are mankind's immortality.

> ... Presences
> That passion, piety or affection knows,
> And that all heavenly glory symbolise. ...

(Of course, in a healthy society, the surviving arts will not be celebrated *at the expense* of the contemporary arts, nor will the contemporary arts be enjoyed to the detriment of the surviving arts.)

The arts so defined — as essentially human and essential to humanity — should hardly need to plead for a place in the education of the young, and in the continuing education of us all. Everyone should have (and most do have) the opportunity to study *and practise* at least one art-form at school. I would go further. A core-curriculum, which makes compulsory provision for the study of (say) mathematics, English, science, a foreign language, should also include one of the arts. Obviously, it is one of the tasks of higher education to train the teachers of the arts for the rest of the educational system. But the need for arts teachers cannot provide the fundamental case for the arts in higher education — any more than the need for teachers of mathematics or English constitutes the sole or main justification for the study of those subjects in higher education.

In fact, higher education has recognized the importance of the arts for many years now — in the case of music, for many centuries. It would be odd if it were otherwise. The arts are concerned with some of the central questions of our human life — questions of value, and of quality: the two important and distinct senses of the word *good*. We have for a long time now permitted and approved the *historical, analytical* and *critical* study of the arts in higher education. That argument hardly needs restating. What is to be considered now is the case for the study of the arts in higher education through *creation, performance* and *practice*. Whether one approaches the planning of higher education from the point of view of student demand, or professional needs, or of value to society (as it is, or might be), the arts have an undeniable claim for a proper place. The place they have at present can (like many things) be explained by history, but it can hardly be justified as a rational scheme. The status quo may be the first consideration in planning, but it should never be seen as more than a point of departure.

Effective planning must start with the practitioners. Not only are they the people who are best informed about the details of their subjects, but they are also the ones who are — or should be — accountable to society for what is done in the name of the arts in higher education. A discussion of means, without purpose, would be lifeless: a debate on purpose, without considering means, is likely to be unrealistic. 'All meaningful knowledge is for the sake of action.'

The concern with means has, however, another aspect. The discussions of course design, course location, assessment, teaching and resources, have in common a concern with the question of *standards*. What kinds of standards should be required at entry, and at completion, of courses in the arts in higher education? How are they to be established and sustained? 'I walk through the long schoolroom questioning....'

The business of higher education is the high culture of the hand and mind: and this is also the concern of the arts. At a time when knowledge seems more and more fragmented, and when theoretical, cognitive and analytical study has developed so powerfully at the expense of the practical and creative faculties, the arts have a major role to play in higher education to restore the balance, to provide integrative disciplines, and to present a model of educational roundedness. Perhaps the fundamental case for the arts in higher education is that they offer institutions and individuals an ideal of wholeness, of integrity, that is nowadays not easily found elsewhere.

> Labour is blossoming or dancing where
> The body is not bruised to pleasure soul,
> Nor beauty born out of its own despair,
> Nor blear-eyed wisdom out of midnight oil.
> O chestnut tree, great-rooted blossomer,
> Are you the leaf, the blossom or the bole?
> O body swayed to music, O brightening glance,
> How can we know the dancer from the dance?

6

The Task of NAB

The National Advisory Body for Local Authority Higher Education in England came into being on 1 February 1982. Its terms of reference at its inception in 1982, and at its reconstitution in 1985 (as the National Advisory Body for Public Sector Higher Education), are given in Appendix A. The Butler Education Act of 1944 describes education as 'a national service locally administered'. As its title suggests, NAB has embodied a compromise between central and local government, and it works. But the early months were not easy.

By the summer of 1982 it had been decided to conduct a major planning exercise for the 400 or so colleges and polytechnics in the public sector. In a sector that was on the defensive and understandably suspicious of the new body, it was difficult to get agreement on the form and details of the proposed exercise. Although we badly needed a strategic framework, it was unlikely that we could decide upon one in the short time available. The invitation to address the conference of the Council of Local Education Authorities at Sheffield in July 1982 provided a welcome opportunity both to report on NAB's early months and to offer in public an outline strategy for the future. In retrospect it is interesting to compare the seven principles (or characteristics) of local authority higher education listed here with the later development of NAB's strategic thinking, as put forward, for example, in the consultative document of 1983 (Appendix C) or the longer-term advice to the Secretary of State in 1984.

This is a provisional and individual report on the first half year of the National Advisory Body, and my own reflections on the tasks ahead of us. They are formidable tasks, and this is by no means an easy time to be setting out on a new and challenging venture in national education. In the present economic climate, with cuts in public expenditure the order of the day, it might seem to some − and not only the faint-hearted − hardly the time to be moving forward to offer, in partnership with the universities on the one hand and the voluntary and direct grant sectors on the other, what we are terming 'a coordinated approach to provision in higher education'. Yet I do not think it at all inappropriate that NAB should have been established and set to work, or that its members are minded to look beyond the short-term programme of retrenchment caused by the cuts in public expenditure to the challenges and opportunities of planning an even more effective and responsible system of higher education for the future.

Let us make no mistake about it, higher education is one of the things we do well in this country. There is plenty of evidence of that. Whether we consider the stream of overseas students (higher education has been one of our major successful export industries), or the way in which institutions abroad seek to employ our academic staff (or borrow them for a year at a time), or how much is achieved in the short span of, for example, a three-year Honours degree, we must conclude that British higher education is a successful part of the nation's enterprise, and something we should all be proud of. And this is (I believe) especially true of local authority higher education which has grown at an astonishing rate in the last twenty-five years, from a time when there were no more than about 34,000 full-time and sandwich students in public sector institutions, and most of those were doing teacher training, to the present time with more than 160,000 full-time and sandwich students, and more than 150,000 part-timers. Consider also the extraordinary range of innovative courses which have been developed and approved and tested successfully since Robbins reported in 1963. At its best, local authority higher education is boldly experimental, cost-effective, quickly responsive to local and national needs, ready to monitor and evaluate its own performance, and of guaranteed quality. And it is to its eternal credit that it is prepared to work at the margins — to extend the reach of higher education, by providing for the late-developer or the mature student, or by exploring and developing new subjects (eg food science and librarianship) and new methods (eg modular degrees and sandwich study). Speaking as a university teacher who has spent half a working lifetime teaching able students on a well-established course, I have for many years half secretly admired the proportionately greater achievements of my colleagues in local authority higher education, and regretted that I too was not working at the growth points of higher education for the future. And now I am.

The main stimulus to the growth of the education system as we know it today came with the passing of the 1944 Education Act which required local education authorities to prepare schemes of further education in their areas. The 1956 White Paper on Technical Education (DES 1956) proposed a substantial increase in the output of advanced courses. After the Robbins Report on Higher Education had recommended in 1963 the granting of university status to the nine colleges of advanced technology, and the establishment of the Council for National Academic Awards, the Crosland White Paper of 1966 (DES 1966) considered the future of the twenty-five regional colleges. It emphasized the importance of a continuing significant local authority stake in higher education and proposed the formation from them of twenty-eight polytechnics (later increased to thirty, of which one is in Wales and, therefore, outside the scope of NAB), which would provide the focus for the development of a distinctive public sector, complementing the universities within a binary system of higher education. This policy, supplemented by the proposals of the 1972 White paper (DES 1972) for the integration of teacher-training with the rest of higher education, created the present, maintained, structure. With the apparent completion of the reorganization of the colleges of education (and after numerous amalgamations, closures and the establishment of a number of free-standing colleges of higher education), the outcome at the moment is a system of some 400 public sector institutions, of which about sixty are major providers of advanced further education (AFE) and a further 100 or so make an important contribution to it, while the remainder are primarily concerned with non-advanced higher education (NAFE), but offer some advanced provision.

The establishment of the National Advisory Body in the early months of this year — four years after the Oakes Report of 1978 — is fresh enough in people's minds to need little rehearsal. The membership of its Committee and Board, their terms of reference, and the first meetings in the Royal Festival Hall in February, will be readily recalled. A monthly cycle of Committee and Board meetings was established at the outset, and five working groups set up to prepare business for consideration by the Board. Three of these were subject groups: for pharmacy, engineering, and art and design; and two were operational working groups: one to look into NAB's data-base and the other to consider the regional aspects of our work. A sixth working group is about to be set up. There have now been five meetings each of the Committee and the Board. What have we achieved?

The Board has helped to stimulate the issuing of DES circular 5/82 (DES 1982), which lifted the moratorium on the planning of new courses, and we have been asked by the DES to look into the question of under-recruiting courses. The outcome of this latter exercise — so far — is a recommendation (from both Board and Committee) to withdraw approval from three courses from September 1982. A further sixty-eight under-recruiting courses will be reviewed during 1982/83, with a view to a possible recommendation for closure from September 1983. At the same time the Board intends to look at three subject areas where questions of under-recruitment have been identified: textile technology, town and country planning and environmental health, and nautical studies.

NAB officers and members contribute to the Joint Technical Group, which is carrying out further work to refine the unit-cost approach to the distribution of the AFE pool and, among a number of other questions, considering the relative weighting of part-time work, about which it is hoped to make a proposal to the Board shortly.

Much time and effort has been spent in (I quote from the Board's terms of reference) 'establishing effective liaison with the university, voluntary and direct grant sectors of HE, with appropriate validating and professional bodies and with representatives of industry and commerce.' The many meetings I have attended have convinced me of the goodwill and encouragement offered to NAB by its neighbours, and I am grateful for the advice and help we have received, and the warm welcome shown to us.

Another immediate concern of NAB is the institutional implications of the forthcoming allocations of teacher training places in the light of advice given by the Advisory Committee on the Supply and Education of Teachers (ACSET). In as far as it is possible, we will help with the concomitant difficult decisions to be faced in the next few months. Meanwhile we have been preparing what has become known as our short-term plan. This is based on three perceptions:

(a) that the public expenditure cuts will impose a 10% (or worse) reduction in the AFE pool by 1984/85;

(b) that NAB must advise on how to accommodate this drastic retrenchment not later than September 1983;

(c) that only an institutional approach will solve the problem.

What is meant by an 'institutional approach' is this. While some of the retrenchment can, no doubt, be achieved in some institutions by further reducing unit costs, a substantial part of it must be met by reducing provision (by amputation, that is, rather than by further slow starvation), and — in some cases — this may mean the total withdrawal of pool funds. It would be easy to share out the 10% cuts equally to all — you wouldn't need a NAB to do that: it could be done across the desk in the DES. But NAB is intended to discriminate. And if we are to discriminate to protect the most valuable work at the expense of what is judged to be less valuable, we must, in logic, expect to cut some institutions by more than the average. We must try to find out where it would be appropriate in an institution to impose a higher than average cut. (If the institutions cannot tell us, we might have to guess — but I hope not, for that would be inefficient and undesirable.) We do not expect very many — if any — institutions to be able to accommodate a full 10% cut by merely cutting unit costs (slow starvation). In most cases, given present projections of public expenditure, some (regrettable) amputation will be required. NAB must try to find out where that amputation will cause least trouble.

For the long term, NAB intends to move forward as fast as possible from a situation where higher education planning is resource-led and system-led to one where educational objectives are the first consideration. Whatever may be true in other spheres of activity, what businessmen call 'the bottom line' is not the appropriate overriding criterion for evaluating the performance of educational institutions. And education planning, while it must (of course) take proper account of available resources, does not take that as the point of departure. Similarly, a system of educational organization should be designed to facilitate education, not to determine it. If we can agree that the first essential in effective educational planning is the definition of objectives, the question arises where that should take place. My own view — and I am not alone in NAB in thinking this — is that all effective planning (including the decisive first step of making an explicit definition of objectives) starts at the grass-roots, within the local education authorities and in institutions among the active teachers, and not at the centre in NAB. It will be enough for the moment for NAB to try to create an environment and a system with stability and continuity enough to enable effective planning, good teaching and sound learning to flourish in the colleges and polytechnics as they should, and to inform the gradual process of creating truly responsive and responsible national planning in local authority higher education. Nevertheless, as our 400 or so institutions consider their answers to the NAB short-term planning exercise, and as they reflect on their own longer-term plans, they will, I believe, do well to bear in mind certain characteristics distinguishing local authority higher education and both adopt them as principles upon which their future work should be founded and use them as touchstones for forward planning. As principles they are not new: others have commented on some (or all) of them often before and they do not all apply – or apply equally – to every LEA institution. But they do represent, in my view, the distinctive importance of the public sector, and they constitute – I shall argue – a reasonable and defensible basis for future planning and development.

First, *local authority higher education is local and regional in emphasis rather than national.* 'Education has been described as a national service locally administered. Its national character is nowhere more marked than in higher education' (Oakes 1978). The national character of local authority higher education, no negligible feature of it, has been appropriately recognized in the creation of NAB. But the emphasis in this sector is and should be a local and regional one, and NAB created as one of its first working groups a regional sub-group to advise on the possibilities of developing an appropriate and effective regional sub-structure which can, like the central body, interact with the universities and voluntary colleges. In the years to come, I believe that institutions (both inside and outside our sector) which lack local and regional roots and links will be at a disadvantage.

The second principle recognizes that, in many institutions in local authority higher education *advanced further education and non-advanced further education form a seamless web*, supporting one another's existence, and benefiting from one another's presence. NAB is responsible only for AFE, but it will not lose sight of the fact that for most of the institutions in its scope, the interweaving of AFE and NAFE is a living and thriving reality. This will make planning exercises even more difficult and, both at the centre in NAB, and at the periphery in the institutions, care must be taken to consider possible 'knock-on' effects upon NAFE of decisions which were intended to affect only AFE. It will be easier to take effective account of this principle in the institutions – where the information is readily available and the risks apparent – than in NAB itself – where the number and complexity of the multifarious interconnections between AFE and NAFE are difficult to take hold of and comprehend. This consideration further justifies the decision to engage at least at the outset in 'bottom-up' planning.

We must also recognize, within the realm of AFE, the range of levels of work. On a 1980 survey base (DES 1980), rather more than half of the students in local authority higher education (54%) were doing technician and other advanced (but sub-degree) courses, while the postgraduate, first degree and teacher training students constituted the remaining 46%. The balance between degree and non-degree students differs in the polytechnics (where about 40% were doing non-degree work in 1980) and the colleges (where non-degree students amounted to 75% of the whole.)

A related – but important point – is the need for the institutions, when they consider their future plans, to build on their own strengths, in terms both of subject and academic content, and of level of work. NAB will I hope be concerned not to give encouragement to what is known as 'academic drift', which occurs when – merely because it is more advanced – degree level work within AFE (and AFE itself in comparison with NAFE) is thought to be more important or superior in some way. Let institutions define, defend and enhance their own individual strengths, and not be tempted constantly to envy and ape their neighbours.

The fruitful coexistence of AFE and NAFE in institutions will, I believe, prove to be one of its strengths in the difficult decade ahead of us, when the downward demographic trends begin to be felt in higher education.

Thirdly — and similarly — a distinguishing principle of local authority higher education is the *mixture of modes, the coexistence of full-time, sandwich and part-time work in the same institutions*. On a 1980 survey basis, the split between FT and S on the one hand, and PT day and evening on the other, was 51% against 49%, though again the proportions are less equally balanced in the polytechnics (FT and S 65%, PT 35%) and in the colleges (FT and S 34%. PT 66%) when considered separately. This substantial element of PT work in local authority institutions must be a major factor in forward planning. It is not likely to reduce. Rather, as the combined pressure of a squeeze on funding and the downward demographic trends come to bear on the FT and S provision, it is more likely that the PT proportion will rise. And, since many of us believe that one of the major challenges in higher education for the remainder of the twentieth century will be how to provide a more adequate programme of part-time and continuing education, the local authority higher education institutions will be well placed to meet that challenge and offer the leadership within higher education to satisfy the need — and they must be ready and willing to do so.

The fourth major principle is that *teaching comes first*. In a DES report of 1967 it is stated: 'the main responsibilities of the polytechnics will be as teaching institutions.' In this respect the public sector has an interesting and real advantage over the university sector, where the 'divided aims' of teaching and research do not always complement and reinforce one another. There is (of course) a place for research in local authority higher education, and NAB will have to turn its attention to the question of developing a research policy before too long. It has not so far proved possible systematically to introduce the 'dual-support' system for funding research into the public sector, and I see little chance of it being done in the foreseeable future. Public sector research is, and will have to be, either self-supporting or what is better described as 'advanced study' — an activity which is (in my view) necessary for and mandatory upon every teacher in higher education. Teaching comes first, and the educational welfare of the students must be our primary aim. But in achieving that aim we must always have regard to the quality of the educational experience — a quality that requires the teachers to engage in advanced study in order to offer good instruction, a quality that must be at risk when the unit of resource begins to fall markedly.

When the Secretary of State first talked to me about the role of NAB, he asked 'Are we giving them a fair deal?' I stupidly asked him who he meant ... 'The students, of course', he said. His was a good question, and if NAB can help to answer it — and answer it in the right way — it will have done its job.

The fifth principle is that *local authority higher education is characteristically — and should be — cost-effective*. The development of a system of unit-cost funding, with its differentiation of three types of subject-work, provides an initial, but crude, measure of the cost-effectiveness of institutions. As the procedure of 'further funding' — a device to ease the transition for historically high-cost institutions — is phased out, or redeployed in a positive way, the public sector will (as a whole) come to share the characteristic of cost-effectiveness. But before that, institutions will need to review their courses carefully, and their student/staff ratios. There is little doubt that some course-design is inherently expensive, with small teaching groups being generated (for example) by means of an over-generous provision of options. Furthermore, the student/staff ratios in some institutions are remarkably low in comparison with practice elsewhere, and need thorough review. The sector will be better able to defend itself when all institutions recognize, and act on the recognition, that planning should be grounded on cost-effectiveness.

Sixth — and in many ways the most important principle to apply to future planning — *local authority higher education is characteristically responsive to need*, whether expressed by student demand, the requirements of employment, or the demands made upon it by the policies and directives of local or national government. Student demand, since Robbins, has been one of the primary determinants of higher education planning, and rightly so. Not only does it determine the *size* of the system, it also *shapes* it, by preferring some subjects (or subject areas) to others, and thus affecting the subject balance. Of course, the approaching decline in the size of the successive 18-year-old age groups will not necessarily require (or justify) a further shrinkage of the system — it would be possible in theory (and desirable in practice!) to attempt to increase the age participation rate when the opportunity is offered. But that issue, fortunately, is still several years away from us: the decline does not start until the mid-1980s, or become steep until the 1990s. In the public sector the very wide age spread of students entering the system and the high proportion of mature students will, for some time, insulate it from the immediate effects of the demographic trend.

More immediate is the question of subject balance. At a time when government policy and received wisdom calls for a decisive shift towards science and technology, forgive me if I sound a note of caution. Student demand is such that now (and for some time) we have had vacant places in science and technology. What students choose to study is determined far more by the choices they make (or are made for them) in school than by the subject provision offered beyond school. Moreover, our students are our customers, and while I wouldn't wish to argue that in higher education the 'customer is never wrong', he may well be right a good deal of the time. Perhaps the aggregated wisdom of many individual student-choices may be superior to the sometimes facile received opinions of this utilitarian age? I do not know. But before we too readily reject responsiveness to student demand in favour of an uncritical responsiveness to the needs of employment, let us be sure we know what employment needs are. Employers I have spoken to are well aware of the 'vocational paradox' and as keen to avoid it as are the students. (The vocational paradox describes the situation where students are carefully trained in an applied subject or on a vocational course — which sometimes takes them down a cul-de-sac, since the relevant employment prospects at the end are poor, and the education they have received appears to disqualify them for any other job.) There is, of course, a need and a place for a large number of specific vocational courses, but they need to be designed — and redesigned from time to time — in close consultation with the relevant employers. It is not clear that in the realm of general education employers necessarily or always want a high level of expertise in science or technology: often they seem to be looking more for holders of final qualifications who are generally well-educated and, while claiming no expertise, are not frightened by quantitative methods or unacquainted with the principles of science and technology.

NAB intends to examine these questions carefully. Our new Industry Group will have the task of advising the Board on what the world of employment really wants. And when that is clearly understood, it will be for the sector to respond. I hope that local authority higher education will continue to demonstrate its adaptability and flexibility and plan for the future with high regard to the principle of responsiveness to defined need.

The seventh, and last principle (at least for the present) that I wish to commend is *the requirement of quality* in all the work of local authority higher education, guaranteed by the rigorous external validation which is one of the most notable — and praiseworthy — features of the public sector. This is not the occasion to discuss the work of the Council for National Academic Awards, the validating universities, the Business and the Technician Education Councils (shortly to merge), and the professional bodies; suffice it to say that the various validating authorities provide an explicit and sound guarantee of a threshold of quality — of acceptable standards — in the majority of the work done in the public sector. (A minority of the work, of course, does not qualify for external validation.) This threshold of quality should provide a springboard from which courses can (and often do) aspire to standards well above it. Institutions and LEAs will do well to take careful account of the principle of quality in their forward planning.

NAB will also itself wish to make judgements of quality. Whether in an era of expansion or contraction, planning must relate to quality — as well as to such factors as the national requirements of subject provision, regional and local needs, the demands of employment, likely student numbers, and available resources. NAB will not find it easy to make judgements of quality. I hope we shall have the co-operation of the validating authorities, of the professional associations and (where appropriate) of the research councils. We shall certainly look to HM Inspectorate for guidance, and we shall from time to time ask the institutions to make their own cases to us. But we shall also have to consider whether (and, if so, how far) it is possible to develop objective and explicit measures of quality in local authority higher education, bearing in mind that these will need to meet the tests of fairness, relevance and practicability.

It will not be to the credit of NAB, however, if it seeks to impose a dull uniformity on local authority higher education. The institutions should continue to play to their strengths, define their own roles, celebrate their individual excellence, and promote and protect their own distinction — in both senses of that useful word. But this must be done, both at the periphery and in the centre, in a spirit of realism. The *status quo* — the single major factor in any planning exercise — is where we must start from, and it will determine to a large extent where we can hope to arrive.

Realistic planning, recognizing the imperatives of the *status quo*, will also prevent us from losing sight of those three great external constraining factors: demographic trends, patterns of employment (or unemployment), and available resources. NAB, I hope, will manage to combine the realism of facing squarely *what is*, with the vision that aspires to *what might be*. We know that our advice will not always be welcome to those who receive it, or who have to bear its effects. But we do not intend to shirk our responsibilities or shun the task. We are ready to answer for the quality of our advice, and we hope that others with responsibilities for local authority higher education will also be prepared to be accountable. We mean business. We do not expect, or intend, to fail. We call upon our partners in the institutions, in the DES, and in the LEAs, to join with us in a common task to protect, preserve and enhance all that is best and most valuable in advanced education in the public sector.

7

Where's the Bloody Horse?

From time to time during the last five years a group of us in Oxford have arranged seminars for invited audiences on current issues in higher education. In 1982 we held a series of such meetings to discuss higher education and Oxford. The collected papers were published in the *Oxford Review of Education*. On this occasion, my task was to speak on the subject 'Higher Education and Oxford: recapitulation and prospects'. As in almost any highly successful institution, Oxford's besetting sin is complacency: the style of this seminar paper was designed to puncture complacency and stimulate a thoughtful response. To that extent it was successful, as the Postscript shows. It is instructive three years later to review the twenty-five propositions voted on at the end. Within Oxford, the following issues have been tackled: 2(b), 2(d), 5(c); others (in one form or another) are currently on the national agenda: 1(a), 1(d), 3(c), 6(a), 6(b) for example. But of the fifteen accepted by the participants, some ten have yet to be followed up. They constitute a programme of reform for the university as desirable and urgent today as it was in 1982.

I have been a member of the University of Oxford – in some capacity or other – for most of the past twenty-five years, and a don for the last eighteen. In reviewing that period I am struck by the difficulty of defining what has been happening – what were important events? or significant changes? or (more common in Oxford) decisive resistance to change? The era begins, for me, with the Franks Report and the Franksian reforms, and although much was then done which one applauded (and still applauds) there were also significant failures to implement the proposed changes: for example, the failure to establish an effective Council of Colleges, or to come to grips with the knot of problems involved in the organization of postgraduate education. Since then, and in no coherent order, we have seen a number of remarkable changes: a strong move to create a university of mixed colleges – which, while it has improved the educational opportunities for women in Oxford, has done little to increase their *professional* opportunities (rather the reverse); we have seen the modern system of joint appointments, which gives ever greater weight to the criterion of productive scholarship, as against effective teaching, for determining the academic staffing of the university and colleges; we have seen the development, following the Kneale Report, of a range of joint degrees, most of which at this stage are judged to be less than successful; admissions has moved firmly away from heads of colleges and from the corporate governing bodies of colleges into the hands of the individual subject tutors, with a profound effect on the criteria used for selection and the expectations we now have of our junior members; we have seen the development and growth of the graduate colleges and the resolution of the non-don problem; we have come to terms — remarkably easily — with the new arrangements for settling college fees, though these (like the joint appointments system) make serious inroads into traditional and long-valued college freedoms; we have seen a definite shift towards providing residential accommodation for both under-graduates and graduates for a substantial part of their career; in short the university and the colleges have grown larger, wealthier and more professional during the 1960s and 1970s. But the party ended in 1981: and we now face, almost to the extinction of any other consideration, the challenge of making in three years a 3% cut in student numbers, and meeting an 8% cut in resources. Others are worse off.

It is easy to see now that what Professor Halsey has called the 'failed thrust' towards higher education at a national level is the necessary context for a review of Oxford's position. The failure to raise the age participation rate, the unpopularity of higher education after the student troubles of the late 1960s, the recognition that there is no direct relationship between higher education (*as it is currently practised in Britain*) and national economic success — nor, apparently between higher education and a more equal society — all these things create a national context where a cut in resources available for higher education must be expected in a time of general resource constraint. It has been possible to argue — so far — that Oxford should be partly shielded from the cuts: it has not been possible to avoid them altogether.

One interesting result of the current painful squeeze is the clearer recognition in Oxford — clearer than heretofore — that the university is part of a national system which is itself merely one part of our remarkable binary system of higher education. The Secretary of Faculties' essay on the UGC/CVCP/NAB and Oxford in this series of seminars is notable not only for its forceful argument and controversial judgements — but because of the detailed interest (shown both in the paper itself and the discussion afterwards) in such external bodies as the University Grants Committee and the Committee of Vice-Chancellors and Principals. Contrast that debate with the inward-looking discussions of Oxford found in the Franks Report and subsequently. Paragraphs 457-459 of the Report briefly discuss what are described as external pressures and demands bearing on Oxford, but the effect on the modern reader is to suggest an era when such pressures and demands could be easily resisted or contained by Oxford. Not so, now. The challenges from outside come more frequently and more threateningly each year — though they often provide a healthy stimulus — last year the DES approach on college fees, this year the UGC cuts, next year (perhaps) a political challenge to our admissions system?

So much for retrospect. But two themes seem to emerge from our discussions of the previous six seminars: the recognition that Oxford's future is closely linked to the availability of resources, and the conviction among many of us that the *existing system* of this collegiate university, with all its peculiar and entrenched traditions, is a major factor in determining what is to happen — or (if you like) will prove to be a major impediment to radical change. We seem to see the future of Oxford as — in the fashionable jargon — resource-led and system-led. This is a bleak prospect — because — and this is my main thesis — no university, no educational establishment, no system of higher education, no nation should undertake its planning on these two bases. What should be the proper basis for planning?

It was Lord Bullock who asked, '*What should Oxford do?*' And we have yet to meet the challenge of that question. We have spent some time considering the idea of Oxford as a model for other parts of the higher education system. It has been argued that Oxford, because of its wealth of resources, its residential tradition, its roots in nineteenth-century ideas of liberal education and its current adherence to ideas of scholarship which are theoretical rather than practical, educational rather than vocational, élitist rather than comprehensive — that Oxford (thus defined) is a dangerous model for others to imitate. The (Oxford) poet Hopkins said of Milton — a Cambridge man — that 'one should admire and do otherwise'. And that, save for the arrogance of demanding admiration, would be my advice to the higher education system of Britain with regard to Oxford — Do otherwise. But it does not follow from that statement that I believe necessarily that Oxford should be other than itself, any more than Hopkins wished to rewrite *Paradise Lost*. So I would dispute the thesis that (to quote an earlier speaker in these seminars):

> Oxford might be termed the flagship for other institutions, but must assume the responsibilities that this position in the vanguard entails. The security it enjoys in comparison with other universities, its undeniable quality, the fact that it benefits from resources available nowhere else, makes it incumbent upon Oxford to give a lead.

Institutions, like individuals (I believe), must work out their own salvation and pick their models with care. So I am not really interested in the answer to Lord Bullock's second question, '*What do other universities want us to do?*' And I fear that if we take it seriously we shall merely produce yet another brake on effective thought and action. The President of Corpus has rightly advised us not to indulge in 'fashionable guilt', and (while we should also strive to avoid 'comfortable complacency') I am inclined to agree with him. Lord Bullock's first question was the right one.

My answer to What should Oxford do? is that we should redefine our objectives, provide adequate incentives for their realization, and monitor the performances of those responsible, and reward success. In other words, our planning should be based initially, not on resources, not on the existing systems, not on administrative convenience, but on a clearly-defined set of objectives. And this definition of objectives should start from the small units — the colleges, departments, sub-faculties and committees. I believe this is the only way of breaking out of the vicious circle — found everywhere in higher education these days — whereby so many of us excuse our own failure of purpose, or inaction, by claiming that we are waiting for some higher authority to tell us what to do, while at the same time resenting the very idea of central management. I have taken the hint for this thesis from the words of the University Registrar – though he is no way responsible for my elaboration of them – when a week or two ago, he said, 'surely we must decide what we want to achieve first, before we consider how to achieve it?' Academics, in my experience, find this very difficult to do: the academic mind would always rather discuss means than ends.

But the trouble with discussing means in preference to ends is that one can never decide whether (for example) the President of Corpus was right when he said that what was needed was 'tinkering, not upheaval'. He may be right, he may not; but only a redefinition of our objectives will give us an adequate basis for judgement. Oxford, after all, is notoriously resistant to change of any sort, whether tinkering or upheaval. And rightly so. Most of us believe – and many shrewd judges outside Oxford share this view – that Oxford is one of the better human institutions that the world has so far produced: this in itself is a powerful argument against change. Moreover, it appears – and the argument has been repeatedly put – that to change any substantial part of the system of this collegiate university would result in further uncovenanted, and perhaps undesirable, changes: a version of the domino theory. When one combines these two powerful conservative forces with a system of government which diffuses and distributes power so that no person and no committee has the opportunity of providing effective leadership, then the obstacles in the way of achieving radical reform from within Oxford are formidable.

The reason why I have taken time to remind you of the powerful forces ranged against the possibility of reform within Oxford is because I believe that Lord Bullock's first question must be answered with a programme that is not only elegant, but also practicable. To be right but ineffective is a great sin. I believe with John Macmurray that 'all meaningful knowledge is for the sake of action'.

So my proposition involves objectives, incentives, monitoring, and reward, starting from the smaller units. To give an example, from my own areas of responsibility, I am suggesting that there should be a defined, public and defensible answer to the questions What are the objectives of Keble College? or What are the objectives of the Honour School of English Language and Literature? Some will answer that 'teaching and research' are the objects of the colleges and the university, but we need still to discuss the appropriate priority to give to each; we need to define and defend the objectives of research in non-utilitarian subjects such as English literature. As for teaching, it is surely time that we attempted to resolve the muddle of a university whose collegiate organization and buildings exemplify an ideal of liberal education for gentlemen, whose academic staff (with few exceptions) are devoted to a scholarly ideal in which research and advancement of knowledge are felt to be more important than the general education of the young, and whose funding comes from a society and a government much more committed to the utilitarian ideal of training manpower for a national purpose. What *are* we up to? This muddle of objectives – which could (and perhaps should) be much more fully elaborated than I have time for is (in my view) the central problem and the central challenge. Lord Franks convicted All Souls College of infirmity of purpose some sixteen years ago: the disease has spread to the whole university – if not wider still into higher education outside Oxford. Our first task is to reconsider what we are about.

The prospects for Oxford depend not a little on whether we have the courage to face this challenge, or not. If so, we might release a new energy which could, as has happened before in Oxford, revivify the university and perhaps also inspire others. If not, then the prospects are depressing, and we can only expect the tribute paid by Roy Campbell to some South African novelists...

> You praise the firm restraint with which they write —
> I'm with you there, of course:
> They use the snaffle and the curb all right,
> But where's the bloody horse?

POSTSCRIPT

It was tempting to end with Roy Campbell's splendid epigram. But the discussion which followed sounded more like the beginning than the conclusion of a seminar. It was encouraging and enlightening to listen to a debate on the objectives of the university and the colleges. There seemed to be two main threads — that we must take a pluralist view of the university, recognizing a variety of appropriate (and reconcilable) objectives, and that undergraduate education in particular had undergone a narrowing of purpose to become highly meritocratic with a very limited definition of success. I do not dissent from either of these propositions.

In arguing that we should set out to redefine our objectives, I have not intended to imply that the task would be easy, nor that we should expect to discover shared aims or a common purpose, or that the multiplicity of goals claimed by the smaller units within the university would necessarily prove complementary or reconcilable. But I still believe that we should consider ends before means, and that we should resist the premature compromise, or 'fudge' whereby the creative tension between contrasting views is too easily and too often sacrificed for an empty consensus.

Undergraduate education in Oxford (and perhaps elsewhere) would, I am sure, benefit from careful reconsideration and redefinition of aims. The competition between colleges for supremacy in the Norrington table, while not in itself undesirable, can lead to a view of undergraduate education which emphasizes high scholarly achievement at the expense of all other considerations, and to a consequential neglect of the educational experience of all but some 20% of our junior members. With the drastic reduction in the opportunities for academic careers it is more than ever essential to plan the education of our undergraduates in less narrow terms.

The seminar ended bravely... The chairman (amid stifled protests) persuaded the two dozen or so present to vote on the following twenty-five propositions. No (further) discussion was allowed: no amendments were permitted: abstention was discouraged. (Readers will note that propositions 2a and 4b were taken, unacknowledged at the time, from the Franks Report.) Whether the propositions were accepted or rejected is indicated after each one.

1 a The present system of tenure in the university should be radically modified. (accepted)

    b The relationship between university and collegiate resources should be reviewed and reformed. (accepted)

    c At whatever cost to existing activities in the university, a small proportion of 'free money' should be set aside each year to fund important new work. (accepted)

    d The balance between 'science' and 'arts' at Oxford should be shifted substantially in favour of science. (rejected)

2 a Oxford should work towards the initiation of plans for the reform of the admissions system on a national scale. (rejected)

    b Encouragement and impetus should be given by the university to the reform of the A level examination system. (accepted)

    c Oxford should recognize the OND and similar qualifications for admissions purposes. (accepted)

    d The post-A level entrance examination should be abolished. (accepted)

    e The Oxford entrance examination should be abolished altogether. (accepted)

    f The post-A level examination should be retained solely for admissions to Commoner places. (rejected)

3 a The balance between undergraduate and graduate numbers at Oxford should be shifted substantially in favour of postgraduate education. (rejected)

    b Oxford should undertake a major review and (if necessary) reform of the arrangements for postgraduate studies in the arts (accepted)

    c Oxford should, at whatever cost to other work, give high priority to the maintenance of the dual support system for research. (accepted)

4 a Oxford should undertake a major review and (if necessary) reform of the college system. (rejected)

    b The General Board, with the co-operation of all the colleges, should at once take steps to establish the relative functions of tutorials, classes, and lectures in the education of undergraduates. (accepted)

    c There should be a thorough review of, and open debate about, the merits and demerits of the tutorial system in Oxford. (accepted)

    d The General Board and each (sub-) faculty should without delay, review the contents of the existing syllabuses in order to ensure *inter alia* that they are not overloaded or over-specialized. (accepted)

5 a Oxford should replace bi-cameral government (Council and General Board) with uni-cameral government. (rejected)

    b Some means should be found to develop a 'Cabinet' to provide central leadership and management. (rejected)

    c A substantial initiative should be taken to secure private funds to supplement the public funding of Oxford. (accepted)

6 a Oxford should work towards the initiation of plans for a credit-transfer system on a national scale. (rejected)

    b The balance between full-time and (part-time) continuing education at Oxford should be shifted substantially in favour of continuing education. (rejected)

    c Oxford should relax its residence requirements. (rejected)

7 a Some means of informal discussion of current issues should be available in the university. (accepted)

b There should be a thorough debate on the merits and demerits of the Final Honours School classification system. (accepted)

8

Dominus Illuminatio Mea

The University Sermon is an Oxford institution. Each Sunday in term a preacher addresses the Vice-Chancellor and Proctors (or their deputies) and a few others on a subject of his choice. At the time when (to my surprise) I was invited to preach the sermon, in St Mary's, the University Church, in the autumn of 1982, I was thinking about the dead hand of inert tradition in our society, the absence of coherent purpose in education, and the life of St Edmund (feast day 20 November) – which I was reading in Aelfric's Old English version with Keble's first-year English undergraduates. Is it really possible (I wondered) to reconcile the principles of rational inquiry and christian faith? Why is there such a resistance to the discussion of christian belief? And does it matter? This (amateur) sermon was a hesitant attempt to answer such questions.

> The lord is my light and my salvation: whom then shall I fear?
> The lord is the strength of my life; of whom then shall I be afraid?
>
> (Psalm 27 verse 1)

What does it mean today for the University of Oxford to proclaim as its motto the words *Dominus illuminatio mea*? I will leave it to historians to explain when and how and why these words were adopted as part of the arms of the university long ago; what, if anything, do they mean for us now? Ancient universities inevitably accumulate over the years an extensive baggage from the past, a luggage of tradition, and though the odd parcel is mislaid as we change trains at successive royal commissions, or sudden self-imposed fits of reform, 'though much is taken, much abides' and Oxford more than most moves forward (or stands still) encumbered (or decorated) by a great burden of tradition – sub-fusc, and the delegates of privilege, and the ancient house of congregation, and the Pass School, and the Clerks of the Market, and matriculation, and 'the triple crown, the open book' with its challenging inscription, and indeed this very University Sermon itself. Oxford seems to carry with it a huge load of inert tradition – like poor Christian's burden in Bunyan's *Pilgrim's Progress*. Does it matter? Does it really matter?

I am inclined to think it does. Tradition, in education as in religion, can be a fruitful ground of inspiration and renewal, can be an anchor, a force for unity and continuity, a refuge and a haven, but it can also be moribund. Inert tradition, in religion as in education, is a slow poison. This is not the occasion to review the traditions of the Church and attempt to decide which are still lively, and which inert: nor am I qualified to do so. And neither is this the time and place for a discussion of the traditions of our University, save one only: what do we mean when we proclaim on the cover of every publication from the Diary to the Dictionary, the words: *Dominus illuminatio mea*? For some individual members of the university, and non-members of course, these words represent a living reality: I hope they do for those who are present now. But as an official claim on behalf of the whole University of Oxford, as a statement — as it were — of university policy, as a touchstone of modern scholarship and teaching, they are not so obviously apt.

Universities today aspire to be — and often are — secular temples of scientific method and rational inquiry. They have thereby enormous achievements of the intellect to their credit, and I should be a fool to deny it, or wish it otherwise, or to imagine that the triumphant progress of science will not continue. But can we really reconcile in one university the honorary degree so justly bestowed on Professor Popper (for example) with the words: *Dominus illuminatio mea*? Or is the christian faith from which the University sprang, and which is still regularly honoured by this University Sermon, no more than inert tradition in Oxford today?

The gulf that seems to lie between the principles of what I have called rational inquiry and the essence of christian faith is I believe more apparent than real. They can, and should, be reconciled — though I concede that it probably has to be done at some cost to either side. But it is surely worthwhile to search for that common ground where faith and rational inquiry can coexist, since not only has each so much to offer the other in co-operation, but also neither of them by itself is enough. Faith without science is rootless, unreal, uncommunicable in the modern world. 'Be ye therefore wise as serpents, and harmless as doves'. The pigeon-brained and sometimes snake-hearted christian has missed the whole point. The long, wrong struggle between the Church and the progress of scientific discovery in the nineteenth century still throws a shadow today.

But, while there are probably few nowadays (and none, I hope in the university) who in the name of their faith would turn away from the disciplines of rational inquiry, there are many more who appear to think that the principles of scientific method by themselves will provide a sure foundation for a university: science is their light. Why do I think that science is not enough?

First, we must all recognize that the process of rational inquiry offers at best a series of ever-closer approximations to the truth. The history of modern thought is filled with examples of triumphant advances in understanding being themselves overtaken and displaced after a time by an apparently better and more complete account of the phenomena in question. Scientists should be humble, and those who pioneer the advances of rational inquiry should be the first to recognize that the best we can hope to do is to make very partial and limited and approximate claims to truth. The christian faith, with its emphasis on humility of life and thought, might seem especially attractive to, and appropriate for, those who devote themselves to rigorous scholarship in universities.

The Church, of course, in its understandable determination to protect and preserve its own best approximations to truth has tended to define humility and selflessness in every way but the intellectual. It is as if we should be prepared to sacrifice everything – cloaks, coats, fathers, mothers – sell all and give to the poor – and follow the way of the cross – but hold on for dear life to our convictions. I do not see it like that, and would remind you of those aweful, despairing words of Jesus on the cross: 'My God, my God, why hast thou forsaken me?' The doubt, the saving doubt, is at the heart of christianity and of science.

The christian faith offers the scholar and scientist a corrective to intellectual arrogance: 'The wisdom of this world is folly in the sight of God'. William Butterfield, the great architect of Keble College (who put chimneys on the chapel – arguing that 'there are bodies as well as souls in the Chapel'), had a vision of the whole life in college: and in the library he inscribed on the window near the law books that great text as a warning to scientists and scholars.

I have argued, first, that faith and rational inquiry can find common ground in intellectual humility to their mutual benefit. My second argument is that, without faith, the processes of rational inquiry provide a means without an end. If we want to discuss – and I do – priorities, values and objectives, we need more than just the rigorous disciplines of rational inquiry. Rational inquiry will show us how to get there, but not where to go. The consequential absence of coherent purpose is one of the most striking and depressing features of our time, both within the nation, within education generally, and even in our own university. I believe that everything that happens should be seen, as far as is humanly possible, as a challenge and an opportunity. And the cuts in higher education resources certainly present us with a heaven-sent opportunity to review our priorities, to restate our objectives, and to redefine our values. Within Oxford the debate seems slow to start; outside, the discussion of fundamental educational issues is sometimes seen as too risky to contemplate. The important questions are not, primarily, about the allocation of resources and the distribution of fees but about the definition of purpose and the establishment of priorities. The issue is not whether to preserve the University Theatre or renew the great organ in this church, for example: an ounce of the faith that moves mountains and a little human ingenuity and energy can, and should, resolve both these problems. The real issue is one of meaning and purpose: what is our university for? And that question cannot be answered by the disciplines of rational inquiry alone: we must also seek 'the true light, which lighteth every man that cometh into the world'.

Scientists recognize that theory is difficult: faith is difficult too. And I am more and more struck by the similarities between the scientific idea of *theory* and the religious concept of *faith*. Science without theory is ultimately meaningless: religion without faith is a contradiction in terms. Here again is common ground. The christian religion which gives so challenging and awkward a prominence to faith has much to offer those who pursue rational inquiry, especially those forms of it (such as the study of literature) which are least informed by theory. The business of a university is not just with thought, but with meaningful thought: it is faith and theory which give meaning to thought. And all meaningful thought is for the sake of action ...

If the illumination offered in the university motto is, as I have argued, intellectual humility, and a definition of purpose and meaning, what has the modern discipline of rational inquiry to offer the Church? Two things, at least, I think. Encouragement towards, first, greater precision of religious statement, and secondly (and similarly) more effective communication with all sorts and conditions of men and women. In particular, it is I believe incumbent upon the Church, both generally – but especially within a university – to make as precisely as possible the distinction between historical truth and legend. This is not an easy distinction to make and sometimes (though rarely) it is not possible to make it with any confidence at all, but in any historical discipline it is a necessary part of the process of rational inquiry to try to do so, and to do so explicitly. Both history and legend contain truth, but the truths – though each may be valuable – are of different kinds, and the distinction is essential and should be unavoidable.

On 20 November, to take but one example, we shall remember St Edmund, King and Martyr, who died in the year 870 in battle against the Danish invaders. The evidence for his sanctity is not compelling. The earliest and most dependable historical record, written within a generation of the events, reports briefly: 'And that winter King Edmund fought against them and the Danes had the victory, and killed the king and conquered all the land.' It is not until almost a century later that the French monk Abbo, after a visit to England, wrote his account of Edmund's life and initiated the growth of the legend of his sanctity. A Church which appears to be careless of the distinction between history and legend in the lives of its saints does not inspire confidence in the accuracy and precision of its more important statements. It cannot expect to be taken very seriously by those who see as fundamental the principles of rational inquiry. Here, most clearly, can be seen the slow poison of inert tradition.

As for communication, I find among people of my own generation and among younger people, a resistance to christian ideas and christian statement that is both interesting and saddening. What is the problem? I do not myself believe it is a linguistic issue: no further official retranslations of the Bible or revisions of the liturgy are needed. Enough damage has been done already to an English christian tradition that was – and still is – anything but inert. The problem is more serious than that: it is one of sincerity. We live in an age and a society that tolerates many evils, but is fiercely and rightly resistant to hypocrisy. I believe that unless the truths the Church wishes to teach can stand the tests of common sense and relevance to ordinary life, the Church will not be heard. All meaningful thought is for the sake of action. And these tests are as important at the institutional level as at the personal. The Church is established, both within the nation and within the university: so long as it remains so established, it must speak with authority and relevance and realism to the nation and to the university.

I urge the possibility – and desirability – of finding and extending the common ground where faith and rational inquiry can coexist and co-operate within a university. Of course the christian message is at once both more momentous, and simpler, than I have been able to explain. Its essence is contained in the diagnosis of the world as a fallen place and the offer of a remedy in the perfect sacrificial love exemplified in the life and history of Jesus. A study of that life provides a syllabus for any university.

9

Economies of Scale

The central concern of a paper I wrote in October 1982 was to relate the theme of 'economies of scale in higher education' to the work of NAB, both in the short and in the longer term. It was given at a conference jointly sponsored by the Higher Education Foundation and the Department of Education and Science, and was later edited by Sinclair Goodlad and published by the Society for Research into Higher Education. It is (with hindsight) interesting to see how our thinking developed from the first outline of the NAB planning exercise (see Chapter 6) to this more detailed account of the problems involved in planning local authority higher education. In particular I note the list of planning criteria and the (intentionally provocative) attempt to offer an order of priority among them. I hoped to start a lively debate. Unfortunately, in 1982 the question that interested people in higher education was not *how* NAB should conduct its planning exercise, but *whether* it could do it at all. (It could — and did.)

My central concern is to relate the theme of 'economies of scale in higher education' to the work of the National Advisory Body for Local Authority Higher Education both in the short and in the longer term. It should be stated at the outset that the views put forward here are personal and do not seek to represent the official policy of NAB.

There are a number of difficulties in addressing the issue of 'economies of scale' which it may be helpful to itemize in order to set them to one side. First of all, there is the question of prejudice; in commenting upon many subjects we are inevitably prejudiced — experience colours thinking. For my own part, for example, I approach the idea of economies of scale inevitably biased by experience in the Universities of Oxford and London (both very large institutions). Although such experience is modified to some extent through other activities, eg by acting as an external examiner for other universities, or by taking part in the validation of degree courses in the public sector, such second-hand experience hardly corrects sufficiently the primary experience of having served for a long time in two very large collegiate institutions. Others will have different experiences, and different prejudices. Secondly, there is the inevitable fact of conscious and unconscious loyalty to one's own institution, which makes it very difficult to recognize that it may not be as economic as it might be. All responsible and responsive institutions mitigate both the social and psychological disadvantages of great size and the financial disadvantages of small size; we can observe easily some of the ways in which this has happened over time. Such a statement begs the question, however, by assuming that there are financial disadvantages from the one, and psychological and educational disadvantages from the other.

It may be self-evident but it is surely true that human beings can in fact make most things work; they are extraordinarily adaptable, as is exemplified by higher education in this country, where people have achieved remarkable (although, perhaps, not very surprising) success in adapting institutions of very different sorts to carrying out a worthwhile job of higher education. It is difficult to think of a convincing example where it could be said that merely because of the size of an institution it is obviously a failure.

The third difficulty in contemplating the issue of economies of scale is the knowledge that to make changes to institutions is costly — not only does it cost money but it is also (often) very costly in human terms. There is nothing new in such a statement: we have all in the last few years watched (or had experience of) institutions being closed and merged in the teacher training rationalization process, and know something about the cost of making large-scale changes to institutions. The universities are now experiencing something similar. We are in general, therefore, predisposed to try to avoid changes — and economies of scale would almost inevitably involve substantial change. The cost of change is always an argument for inertia; whilst it may be a good argument it nevertheless inhibits consideration of the issue.

It is important to clarify whether we are concerned to take up the details of the problem on a *tabula rasa* basis, or to contemplate British higher education as it is, in all its awkward and interesting diversity. On the *tabula rasa* basis it must be recognized at the outset that economies of scale for an institution have to be approached first and foremost through defining the *role* of that institution. Is it a teaching or a research institution or, perhaps, a mixture of the two? The three possible answers here immediately lead to different views about economy of operation. Then, the *level* of work offered by an institution of higher education must be defined — be it sub-degree, first degree, or postgraduate — and one should note the tremendous variety and mixtures of levels available (notably) in the local authority sector, including, most importantly, non-advanced further education. Having defined the level of work one should perhaps go on to define *mode* of study — full-time, sandwich, part-time or a mixture of these three; and then to define the *faculty range* of an institution. This latter point must be a decisive planning consideration; economies of scale will look very different once this question has been answered.

We are rarely, however, in a position to plan the whole of a new university or institution of higher education, let alone a totally new system. Even when a new institution has been planned in this country (for example Keele University or the five later new English universities) the constraints of the prevalent model appear to have been very strong. There seems to be a pressure (either implicit or explicit) which encourages institutions to conform to the norm of size which operates across the system as a whole: the effect of the predominant model is extremely influential and should not be underestimated. The institution-wide desire to conform often leads to a failure to ask or answer questions of principle about organization and size.

Touching briefly on the appropriate size of management structures *at the system level*, the question of how large and how extensive the higher education system as a whole should be in the United Kingdom, I draw attention to the curious sectoral system of higher education in this country. There is the sector constituted by the universities and funded by the University Grants Committee; there is the other (English) local authority sector (with NAB in its advisory capacity); and the DES, with the voluntary colleges and direct grant institutions, constitutes yet another sector, not to mention the Advisory Body for Local Authority Higher Education in Wales, the Scottish Education Department, and Northern Ireland. It is perhaps not unreasonable to question whether these are appropriate management structures at the system-wide level!

Turning to that which is properly the concern of NAB, I note that some people have questioned whether it is actually possible to offer intelligent planning to a sector containing approximately four hundred institutions whilst retaining local education authority responsibility and control; the success (or otherwise) of the NAB will go some way to answering this question. A further question which has quite rightly been raised relates to whether NAB and the UGC (representing the two major sectors of higher education) can co-operate intelligently to avoid the waste and overlap which is believed to occur at the local level (although the extent of wastage which occurs through failure to co-operate − or indeed to inform − across the binary line is not at all clear); these are important and critical questions but not, however, ones to which any answers are offered here.

Moving from the level of the system to that of the institution, one wonders whether it would be possible to achieve the ideal or optimum size of an institution − or for that matter of a department, or indeed a sector − assuming that the ideal size could be agreed upon. It is not reasonable to expect that anything of this nature can be done *in the short term*, but if there were a clear idea of what were the economies of scale, and the most cost-effective as well as the most educationally, socially and psychologically effective size of an institution or department or sector, it might be possible to move towards this *over time*. It must be fairly obvious that if there were such a model, it would not be anything very precise − 4000 full-time equivalent students or something like that − and it would have to be a range. One such range has already been offered by Christian Schumacher with his idea of institutions of not less than 1500 and not more than 4000 students. In approaching the problem of economies of scale many people must surely start from the essentially commonsense position, supported by the Verry and Davies findings (Goodlad 1983), that there are economies of scale in universities and that these are never exhausted, ie that average costs fall indefinitely as student numbers rise.

Such a view would seem to justify the large institutions − but not the small ones. Should the UGC and NAB make their decisions and give their advice to the government on this basis? It would seem at first glance to represent a coherent and sensible position as long as one could take account of the social and psychological problems. An important counter to this argument, however, is that in the local authority sector of higher education at least −

when one moves away from common sense and theory to practice or the reality of the situation – one is surprised to find that economies of scale operate to some degree in the opposite direction to theory. Local authority higher education to some extent has offered a picture of a reverse economy of scale: on a unit cost basis, some of the larger institutions are distinctly more expensive than the smaller ones. Looking at the universities, it is also true that some large universities appear costly on a unit cost basis whereas some small universities appear to be operating very economically. The theory of economies of scale does not appear to correspond in any great degree with the realities of British higher education, and it is the realities with which we have to deal.

A further aspect of the reality of local authority higher education which cannot be ignored is the vitally important fact of non-advanced further education. In the sector for which NAB exercises responsibility, a large number of the four hundred or so institutions are mixed in the sense that they are engaged in both advanced (AFE) and non-advanced further education (NAFE) – and there are good educational arguments for having such institutions.

NAB is in difficulties here, however, in applying the concept of economies of scale; if it is applied from the point of view of AFE it will simply not impact sensibly upon the institution itself. Unlike the UGC, NAB is very often constitutionally concerned only with *parts* of an institution, ie the AFE part, which makes it extremely difficult to apply any crude measure of economies of scale to institutions overall. NAB must bear in mind constantly that economies of scale which might be desirable in terms of AFE could substantially affect important work in the NAFE sector.

In considering the short-term problem of readjusting the system to accommodate the cuts, NAB started from three principles which I would wish to defend very strongly, even though (as with any principles) there are costs involved. The first principle to be adopted was that in the planning exercise (for 1984/85) it was proper 'to ask institutions first' – ie to adopt a bottom-up approach. Although clearly the process has to be an interactive one, it is necessary to start somewhere and it was agreed that the best way was to ask the institutions what they thought should happen to them under certain resource constraints, which were fairly easy to define. NAB – in as much as it is the central planner – would then take a second look and design a 'national plan' on the basis of their views and priorities. It would of course have been possible to do it the other way round – to design a 'national plan' to which institutions would have to accommodate themselves – but it was decided as a matter of principle to adopt the first approach and it is one which NAB would wish to defend. There are costs involved: institutions have been asked to confront some very hard questions, but the important issue is whether (as I believe they do – and should) institutions really want to be able to govern themselves. Self-government involves responsibility for making hard decisions.

Secondly, NAB realized from the beginning, though the implications of this may still not be clearly understood by everybody, that it could not undertake its short-term exercise on a subject basis; it would have to be undertaken on an institutional basis. The recent UGC exercise typifies the subject-based approach. The UGC reviewed subject provision through forty-four universities, and was able to do so because it had a developed sub-structure of subject boards, it knew the institutions well, there were only forty-four of them and there were experienced members of staff who had been in post at the UGC for a long time. In contrast, NAB started its life in February 1982 with no staff, no offices, no working groups and with only half the funds of the UGC. Even if it had been possible to develop a subject sub-structure in the time, the funds were not available to finance it. In addition, the curriculum range in local authority higher education is wider than that in the university sector and would require a wider and much more complex subject sub-structure. Planning in the local authority sector, at least in the short term, has to be done on an institutional basis, and by making institutional decisions. The painful implications of an institutional approach should be clearly understood: any cuts which have to be made will be of institutions or parts of institutions. Unless NAB were to come to the conclusion that the right thing would be to apply an 'equal misery' cut at roughly 10% on every single institution (and it seems unlikely that this will be – or should be – the outcome), the inescapable logic of the two principles sketched out above demands and leads to a selective or discriminatory approach in the application of the overall cuts in resources.

The third principle concerns timing. NAB was brought into existence in February 1982 and was immediately faced with a challenge: could it impact in any real way on the 1983/84 pool allocation? There was never much chance of NAB being able to complete a detailed exercise by the Autumn of 1982, which is when advice to the Secretary of State was required for the distribution of pool funds for 1983-4. The next real question therefore was whether or not the submission of advice to the Secretary of State should be left until 1984, to impact on the 1985/86 pool allocation. An inescapable conclusion in thinking about the latter time-scale was that the cuts would already have happened! In terms of the timing, NAB had very little choice – there was only one year left in which advice could sensibly be offered to the Secretary of State on the allocation of a reduced AFE pool. NAB has to give its advice by Autumn 1983; this timescale was enforced not chosen. If it is thought that 1983 will be too early for NAB to be able to do anything more than rough justice to the system, the responsibility for this lies not primarily with NAB but rather with the timetable within which it is required to work. What criteria can be applied in the very short timescale outlined above? A number have loomed very large in the thinking within NAB and one of its tasks is to give priority to these. The following section offers a personal attempt to order the priorities.

First, there is the question of regional distribution and the likely impact upon this of decisions within NAB for major institutional changes. There will be cases where the issue of regional distribution of higher education will override other criteria which might have led NAB to advise that pool funding be withdrawn from a specific institution. Any short-term rationalization of the sector must have due regard to this question. Second, there is the question of the national importance of work which is being offered within the sector. Is, for example, engineering more important to the nation than leisure studies? Certain things must follow in terms of NAB's short-term plan from the answer to such a question and it is a prime example of one of the key issues which must be tackled. Third, there is the question of the impact of decisions about AFE on NAFE. Here NAB will need to depend on the advice of the regional advisory councils and HM Inspectorate. Fourth, there is quality. How is this going to be assessed? NAB is asking HMI and the validating bodies for advice and help, although it is not yet clear whether the validators will be able to give an appropriate answer. The criterion of quality comes relatively low down in my list of priorities largely because it is such a difficult indicator to measure; it is no use having a criterion if it cannot be applied. Fifth, and last, there is the question of cost-effectiveness, and thus of economy of scale. It is interesting that the criterion which was my central theme should come at the bottom of the list but it should be emphasized that it is a list relating to the implementation of the short-term as opposed to the long-term work of NAB.

There are of course other criteria which are perhaps as important as the five already given, if not more so. There is, for example, the question of the maximum tolerable rate of change within institutions. Higher education institutions cannot change very fast and remain effective — the impact and constraint of a typical three-year degree course is only one example here — and this relatively low, maximum, tolerable rate of change is a severe constraint which (perhaps) leads one to the conclusion that institutions should not be asked to change dramatically in the short term — rather they should continue relatively unaffected or disappear altogether.

The most urgent task which has faced NAB therefore is to advise on the implementation of a 10% reduction in the real level of resources available to local authority higher education, by the autumn of 1983. In so doing NAB must seek to determine how much of this reduction can legitimately come out of unit costs — ie how much 'fat' still exists in the system — and how much has to be achieved through excision of provision. The response from institutions to the short-term planning exercise is crucial in reaching a judgement between squeeze and excision; it is, however, generally accepted that there will have to be a certain amount of amputation in the system, although the extent has yet to be determined. As already noted above, the interdependence between AFE and NAFE is such that a 10% reduction cannot (for example) be achieved by excising all the minor providers from the system. Neither, it should be remembered, are minor providers very costly; it is the major providers which are (often) less cost-effective within the local authority system. This situation suggests that in order to achieve part of the 10% reduction, withdrawal of all AFE pool funding from one or more institutions may have to be recommended. In terms of a major provider this would obviously indicate closure of the institution. How should NAB's advice be framed? Should such an institution be closed? or merged with another, neighbouring institution? The traditional answer to such a dilemma has been that of merger, but is this, in the short term, correct? Mergers create multi-site institutions which take some years to develop their own methods and working relationships; they are, however, socially and politically more acceptable than outright closure and it may be that for these reasons the advice from NAB will lean towards them. Whatever the solution, it will lead to cessation of work and this will inevitably raise the question of redundancies; money cannot be saved without saving on staff. This is a critical issue which needs to be faced squarely.

Equally, however, all the solutions must also raise the question of the control of student numbers. Can the local authority sector for much longer continue to be the part of higher education which has no effective control over numbers? There are no effective means at present, and will whatever means are eventually found contribute to economies of scale? It must be clear that economies of scale, as a concept, is not really helpful to the short-term task facing NAB. It may be more so in the longer term but much more research is needed, not least to show why the theory of economies of scale and the facts of British higher education do not always correspond.

10

Extravagant Hopes
for the Future?

The National Advisory Body – the First Year, theme of the seventh annual Royal Festival Hall Conference on Higher Education, organized by North East London Polytechnic in December 1982, provided an opportunity both for a post-mortem and for some speculation on future development. I was asked to look beyond 1984, the target year for the planning exercise – which explains why I began and ended with a reference to George Orwell. Towards the end I outlined a programme of work for NAB – and for higher education in general. Since 1982 all the issues identified then have been tackled, but much work still remains to be done; with regard, for example, to binary policy or the 'seamless web', or the centralizing tendency in educational management.

Indeed, looking back some two years later, I am struck by the contrast between those issues we have grappled with effectively in NAB (eg research policy) and those we have – perhaps temporarily – lost sight of, such as distance learning. At that time I was becoming increasingly aware that we would find it more and more difficult to achieve our educational objectives without some effective forum for the integrated planning of higher education. This thesis is elaborated and repeated in several of the following chapters. And in 1985, as we await the appearance of the Green Paper on Higher Education, it remains a major unresolved problem. *Either* we must create a new 'overarching body' to direct and control at the strategic level the work of the UGC and the NAB, *or* – a more plausible solution – the DES should be encouraged to take that responsibility to itself. I can see no other answer. Nature abhors a vacuum.

The discussion following the paper at the time was (understandably) defensive and cautious, but at the end of 1982 I was not unhopeful for the future. Nor am I now.

To the future and to the past, to a time when thought is free and men are different from one another and do not live alone, to a time when truth exists and what is done cannot be undone. From the age of uniformity, from the age of solitude, from the age of Big Brother, from the age of double think, greetings.

In Winston Smith's diary, George Orwell offers this grim vision of 1984; we however are fortunate not to live in an age of uniformity, solitude or double think, and I believe that this is in part at least due to our diverse system of education. It is to education — a national service, locally administered — or perhaps to higher education in particular, that we must look to preserve a society where thought is free, where men are different from one another and do not live alone, where truth exists and is fearlessly proclaimed.

I take this as my starting point because I believe it is with firm purpose that we must begin our thinking for the years after 1984/85. We must not begin from external constraints or demographic failures, in terms of employment and unemployment, or from the availability of resources; we must *re-define*, *re-present* and *re-defend* the purpose of higher education. The real challenge to the polytechnics and colleges, to the universities, to the National Advisory Body and to the University Grants Committee, is not to learn to live with reduced resources, difficult though that is and will be; it is, rather, to restate and justify purpose and, in a society which seems dangerously ready to over-simplify such issues, to defend and assert the importance and value of practical and theoretical research, of vocational training and liberal education, and of the enlargement of access and the maintenance of standards in higher education. It must be the task of all of those with responsibility for the planning of British higher education to convince government and society that these aims are all worthwhile and all achievable, given goodwill and intelligence.

An approach to the redefinition of purpose must start wih the question of *demand*. Here there is an obvious distinction to be made between demand from students and demand caused by the needs of employment. Access to higher education has been and will continue to be of significance in the years to come in two different aspects. First, because of the challenge that we face from the need to provide second chances and better opportunities for people to continue their education. Credit transfer has been on the agenda for too long; it is now time for action. NAB has set up a working group specifically to investigate the topic, and hopes to co-operate effectively with the UGC in considering the need for continuing education on a transbinary basis, seeing this as one of the major challenges in the next few years and — for the local authority sector in particular — for the remainder of this century.

Secondly, there is the question of access for the 18+ age group — the subject that all in higher education are well versed in and have been grappling with since the Robbins Report. The question immediately arises as to whether the Robbins principle can be preserved at a time when resources are being drastically reduced. Local authority higher education has a good record in responding to the needs of students as defined by demand from the 18+ age group and I believe that the sector will continue to do its utmost in the years to come to take every possible step to maintain the provision of higher education opportunities for all those 18-year-olds who are able, willing and appropriately qualified.

At present the age participation rate of 18-year-olds in higher education is some 12-13%. There are many countries, some of them our competitors, which achieve a far higher participation rate in terms of entry to higher education and it must be a question for serious consideration whether we should seek to achieve the same. In addressing this issue, NAB will need to consider carefully the dilemma which arises between the need to maintain the unit of resource for students following courses of higher education (in order to ensure the quality of provision) and the need to provide for additional access. I hope that NAB will not move hurriedly to advise upon the reduction of access by the imposition of student numbers control and, before that happens, will explore other solutions.

The first, and to me the most obvious, other solution is in re-designing courses to make them more streamlined and more economical. Secondly, we must investigate very carefully the possibility of stretching student/staff ratios; in some areas at least there is surely still room for more students to be accommodated within existing ratios. Thirdly, I believe that we should review the existing balance between two-year and three-year initial courses of higher education, to see whether this would provide a sensible way of increasing access. This concern to increase access has underpinned the NAB Board's consideration of its discussion paper, 'Towards a Strategy for Local Authority Higher Education in the Late 1980s and Beyond,' and has resulted in the decision of the Board and Committee to issue the paper as a consultative document in order to gain as wide a range of opinion and advice as possible. We very much hope that the debate will be conducted on both sides of the binary line and that it will seek to address the central question of whether it would be appropriate or advisable to seek to offer a limited increase in access through a shift in the balance between two-year and three-year work. This issue is very much at the heart of NAB's longer-term thinking, certainly post 1984/5, but it is for the higher education system as a whole, on both sides of the binary line, to debate the issues and to decide whether or not this would be an appropriate strategy to follow. Provision for students is the key issue here and at the end of the day the maintenance of institutions and their perceptions of their status cannot be allowed to be more important.

Continuing education, opportunities for the 18+ age group, and the two-year/three-year balance are the three things which I believe we need to explore in order to see whether we can maintain and indeed go beyond the Robbins principle. We must also, however, explore every possibility of securing the extra resources that may be needed in the short term in order to do so. In the longer term, demographic trends will begin to take effect, but not significantly until towards the end of the decade. If a genuine extension of access were to take place in the next decade, then the demographic trend would be cancelled out.

Having considered briefly the issue of demand from students, it is important to consider also demand from employers. This has been and will remain a central concern of local authority higher education and NAB has set up a working group to look into the whole question and advise the Board and Committee accordingly. Central to that review will be the question of the balance between more and less vocationally oriented courses both within the local authority sector and within higher education generally. I am not yet convinced that effective manpower planning in higher education can be achieved from the centre; I believe it is better to leave it to the grass roots to review with the local community and industry the needs of employment and the ways in which higher education can meet them. This is clearly, however, a crucial area for NAB and it will have to consider carefully to what extent it should bring to bear, more actively than at present, planning derived from employment demand. Whilst it is a clear duty of higher education to consider the needs of employment and to seek means to meet them, it must also be a question of balance and of emphasis, not of revolution. Higher education must strive to meet and reconcile the needs and demands of students and employment.

Moving on from the issue of demand, and looking beyond 1984/85, I am acutely conscious of the *seamless web of education*. I believe that NAB will have to take even greater note than it has done already of the continuity of secondary education, non-advanced further education and advanced further education, and in this respect the role of the local education authority is of crucial importance. Here there is also clearly a relationship with the issue of access; if higher education is to improve its rate of access it must take steps to consider the problem of the 16-18 year-olds and to look beyond the narrow needs of higher education. Similarly, we must review the effects of the examination system on the curricula and ask whether in doing our own job in higher education as best we can we are making other people's jobs more difficult.

Meanwhile, I hope that in 1984, and after, the partnership which has already begun to develop between NAB, the UGC and the voluntary and direct grant sectors of higher education will be strengthened, and that we will see the development of a *single but plural system* of higher education. This leads inevitably to a discussion of the existing binary line, which it is particularly important to define. In my view the binary line consists of five interwoven strands which together differentiate the two major sectors of higher education: these are local authority responsibility, course approvals, control of student numbers, the role and funding of research, and external validation. I believe that one or more of these strands will be changed and relocated after 1984/5.

Looking at the possibilities of convergence, it is clear, for example, that as NAB moves towards offering the idea of programme planning and programme funding and, ultimately I hope, persuading the Secretary of State to move from course approvals to programme approvals, so the UGC is beginning to interest itself in determining the areas of work to be carried out in different universities. Control of student numbers is another area in which the present position (where numbers are rigidly controlled in one sector and not in the other) cannot continue indefinitely and where I firmly hope that the two sectors will come together. The vision I have is that some of the strands in the binary line will be seen to be unimportant and will fade away. There are three, however, which cannot I think be put to one side: they are external validation, research support, and local authority responsibility. I believe that they will, and should, remain; there is no reason however why they should continue to distinguish one side only or remain drawn where they now are. In the years beyond 1984/5 I hope that we shall be able to consider whether they do fall at the right point.

I believe that the diversity which we badly need in this country will be achieved better by a single but plural system of higher education than by a confrontation between two monolithic sectors. In order to achieve this, institutions must be prepared to *define, restrict* and *defend* their roles. At the centre, the UGC and NAB, together with the Department of Education and Science and the local authorities, must co-operate to relax the binary tension, to redefine the appropriate points at which the remaining, necessary, formal differences have to be drawn, and to review and re-present further and higher education to the nation.

I hope that NAB will in 1984/5, and after, continue to strive to delegate decisions wherever possible and, where it would be advantageous to do so, I would like to see NAB, the central planning authority, decentralized wherever possible. I hope thereby that we may be able to liberate initiative, encourage responsibility, and develop confidence at the level of the institutions and within institutions. The establishment of a three-year planning horizon is essential to the achievement of this aim and is one of the major longer-term objectives of NAB. Some parts of the system complain of too much control and sometimes refer to interference by central and local government. Is such a criticism fair? Would corporate status help? These are questions to which we will have to find answers before the end of 1984/5. NAB itself is a new level of control, and we must seek to avoid the charge of being just another external irritant to the work of the local authorities and institutions. Unless we can liberate initiative, we cannot hope to encourage responsibility and develop confidence within institutions of higher education.

In attempting to look forward beyond 1984/5 I can only pretend to see through the glass darkly; I have suggested that local authority higher education, in partnership with the National Advisory Body, will need to do the following things: redefine aims and purpose; reconsider student demand both in the 18+ age group and in the area of continuing education; consider the demand from employment; recognize more clearly the seamless web of education running through secondary and non-advanced to advanced further education; develop an even closer partnership with the other sectors of higher education; review and refine the binary policy; and maintain and enhance a style of operation which is open, consultative and, as far as possible, decentralized. It will, I feel sure, be faced with demand for further dynamic change and I am confident that it will meet the challenge. Edmund Burke, in his 'Thoughts on the cause of the present discontent', said: 'To complain of the age we live in, to murmur at the present possessors of power, to lament the past, to conceive extravagant hopes for the future, are the common dispositions of the greatest part of mankind.' I do not conceive extravagant hopes for the future but I have firm confidence in the local authority sector of higher education and a belief that, with the help of the educational system in general, George Orwell will be proved if not wrong then premature.

11
The Leverhulme Report

At the Commonwealth Universities Conference, held at Birmingham University in August 1983, the subject of the address I gave was SRHE's Leverhulme programme of study into the future of higher education (see Chapter 5). I dwelt, in particular, upon the general conclusions and recommendations of this wide-ranging inquiry as summarized and presented in its final report, *Excellence in Diversity* (Leverhulme Report 1983). The occasion provided an opportunity to point up some of the report's more challenging criticisms and controversial proposals before a captive audience of vice-chancellors and registrars from both UK and Commonwealth. It seemed too good a chance to miss — but I sensed that those who listened did not really think that the Leverhulme arguments applied to their institutions, or that the concerns of the National Advisory Body were relevant to the universities. Yet the nine questions I posed then still provide a fairly comprehensive agenda for higher education (on either side of the binary line), and the unnumbered final question still remains to be answered.

'For some years there has been no coherent national policy for higher education.' Thus the Leverhulme Report. The Leverhulme Report is timely, I suggest, because it emphasizes the absence of an agreed, coherent policy, sets the agenda for debate and tentatively offers a way forward towards a new strategy for higher education. Any such strategy must take account of the external constraints: demographic trends (including the significance of some stagnation of participation during the 1970s), patterns of employment and unemployment, and availability of resources. The Leverhulme Report is rooted in a serious analysis of these factors, together with a lively sense of the existing distribution of higher education institutions in the United Kingdom in all their complexity. (The major constraining factor on any forward planning, after all, is the *status quo*). It is interesting to compare the carefully worked out Leverhulme strategy with the indications contained (for example) in the Secretary of State's letters to the University Grants Committee in 1982 and to the National Advisory Body in 1983, or with NAB's own discussion document, entitled 'Towards a Strategy for Local Authority Higher Education in the Late 1980s and Beyond'. What all these share is a sober and clear-sighted appreciation of the probable realities of the external constraining factors, realities different from those which affected the Robbins Report. The context has changed, and so must the strategy.

I propose to select and highlight some of the more important issues in the Leverhulme Report, to indicate in what ways (if any) NAB has tackled them, and to suggest some awkward questions they give rise to.

The first sections of the report deal with background, scope and the aims of the strategy. The definition of higher education for the purposes of the programme of study was not easy: there is 'a reciprocity between higher education and the schools, and an infinite gradation between the most academic higher education and the most utilitarian further education' (p.2). The definitions adopted embraced some 450 or so institutions, universities, polytechnics, Scottish central institutions, and other colleges and institutes of higher and further education. What is striking is the diversity of institution-type and the range of educational activity that is included, reminding us constantly to beware of assuming a narrow, stereotyped model of higher education. Not all of it is specialized 3-year Honours degrees for full-time 18+ students living away from home; nor should it be. One of the merits of the report (I believe) is its insistence on relating higher education to the rest of the education service. NAB, which is responsible for local authority higher education, has within its scope the twenty-nine English polytechnics, some sixty or so other major colleges and institutes of higher education, and more than 300 colleges of further education which undertake some proportion of advanced (higher education) work alongside their non-advanced further education. NAB's links with local authorities, its concern with the interface between advanced and non-advanced further education, and with initial teacher training and in-service teacher training, means that it never loses sight of the truth that higher education is but a part of British education. Those of us who represent the universities, however, might ask ourselves the following question:

1 Is university higher education playing its full role as part of the education system, or does it tend at times to stand aside and ignore the continuum of education, 'the seamless web'?

The aims of the Leverhulme strategy (p.4) are of great importance; they are, in brief, to *encourage access*, to *reduce specialization*, to *maintain quality*, to *stimulate research*, to *promote institutional development plans*, to *develop responsiveness*, to *increase efficiency*, and to *encourage leadership*.

I will leave you to decide whether these aims are worthy, coherent, and realistic. I think they are. Some have questioned, however, whether it is appropriate to lay down explicit aims for higher education, or for education generally. The dangers of caging a song-bird are well known, and any list of objectives can − over time− become cramping and constricting. Nevertheless, in the absence of the competitive discipline of the market place, it is important for us to define explicit educational objectives so that evaluation of performance is possible. Just as the Leverhulme Report bravely defines its strategic aims, to make it possible to judge whether its strategic proposals are appropriate, so we suggest that all institutions should prepare realistic development plans, so that their performance can be evaluated.

Perhaps the central issue in the planning of higher education at present is whether we should adopt a centrally-planned model or a market-controlled system. Whether one considers the needs of continuing education, or the aims of stimulating research, or the efficient use of resources, the question is whether these things will be best achieved through central planning and direction, or through setting institutions free to compete in an open market. The Leverhulme Report sees merit in both approaches and recommends a compromise, and a balance, between them.

The first issue it concerns itself with is access. There are a number of related questions here. First, how does access to higher education in Britain compare with that in other advanced societies? Second, what is the balance of access, as between 18+ school-leavers and mature (probably part-time) students? Third, are there any disturbing imbalances in the pattern of access — for example regionally, or in relation to ethnic minorities, or women, or (most serious perhaps) between different social groups? Fourth, and to me most interesting, what are the educational limits to access to higher education? — what proportion of our society could derive benefit from it if there were no other limits to access whatsoever? — how flexible is access? Comparisons with other countries are notoriously difficult to make: but there is some evidence, which I have studied, and which has been used by Ministers in Parliament, to suggest that on the basis of certain assumptions the proportion of the country gaining access to some form of higher education does not compare unfavourably with our competitors in Western Europe or North America. The assumptions of course, are crucial. Amongst others, they include the principle that the appropriate comparison should be based on a count of *new entrants* to *all forms* of higher education: and so course-length, and drop-out, are excluded from consideration; and part-time entrants become equivalent to full-time ones. A comparison at 18+, which allowed for course-length and drop-out, and weighted part-time students appropriately, would tell a different story. But, if as a nation we are to rest our international comparisons so heavily on the part-time student, we should consider, as the Leverhulme Report suggests (p.5) whether 'too much of our higher education effort — and resources — are concentrated on full-time Honours degree courses or school-leavers.' But the second question I have is a different one:

2   What are the appropriate educational limits we should place on access to higher education?

A century or so ago we were considering how far it was appropriate to extend elementary education in our society. In retrospect that seems an odd debate. We now believe that there is no limit. Everyone should have access to, and may benefit from, elementary education. We must now engage in a similar debate, not only about further education, but also about the limits of higher education. I do not believe we have nearly reached them yet. Access to higher education — and this may be particularly true of mature and adult (potential) part-time students — may turn out to be as flexible as policy-makers choose to make it.

The pages of the report dealing with content and structure of courses develop a critical review of the prevailing model of higher education, the specialized 3-year Honours degree. This was my own higher education and I am naturally prejudiced in its favour. But we must beware lest 'one good custom should corrupt the world'. The criticism of the over-specialization and length of the basic building-block of the system must be read not only in the light of one's own (perhaps prejudicing) experience, but also with an eye to Bruce Williams' counter-arguments (pp. 34-5). The main report proposes a radical change, in the general introduction of less specialized, 2-year initial courses. It is interesting that somewhat similar ideas are proposed for consideration in a Council for National Academic Awards policy paper and in NAB's discussion document, 'Towards a Strategy for Local Authority Higher Education in the Late 1980s and Beyond'. Relating questions of access to questions of course structure, the NAB document argues:

> To seek to balance answers to questions about individual access and employment related needs within resource constraints is neither new nor easy. It is desirable, however, that NAB should attempt the exercise in the interest of the sector it is intended to serve. One possible synthesis offers itself, if access is to be maximised while allowing employment related needs to influence provision to a greater extent. If more students took all, or some, of their higher education part-time; if more students lived at home; if a greater proportion of initial courses of full-time higher education were shorter rather than longer: then conflicting demands on the system could be met.
> This is, of course, only one synthesis: there are many others. An obvious alternative, not automatically to be ruled out, is to continue with the present pattern of provision but − in the absence of more resources − to reduce access. Or, if the balance of courses is not to be changed, but access is to be protected, patterns of working involving a different academic year and greater utilisation of teaching accommodation (presumably at some cost) might be introduced. The circle cannot be squared: given the resource constraints, then unless the pattern of provision is modified, the alternative to a reduction in access is a wholly unacceptable deterioration in quality.

The circle cannot be squared; the problem will not go away; the issue must be faced. I suggest the following questions for consideration:

3 Should the present balance between 3 (and 4)-year degree courses and 2-year diploma courses be varied? And if so to what extent? (At present, most of the 2-year work is done in local authority institutions, and much is vocational in nature.)
4 Within any such view, what should be the balance between general courses and more specifically vocational ones?

The next major section of the report (pp.13-15) deals with 'peer review and the maintenance of academic quality', and puts forward two broad views. One is that the non-university institutions (the polytechnics and the colleges) should have less external intervention in their academic affairs: the other that the universities should have more. The quality of the academic provision in polytechnics and colleges is the responsibility, not only of the institutions, but also of HM Inspectorate and the validating bodies (the

Council for National Academic Awards and the Business and Technician Education Council and the validating universities). I believe — after many years experience — that external validation and inspection maintains and enhances academic standards in local authority higher education and in the voluntary colleges. I also believe that all higher education institutions have a duty to give an explicit and defensible guarantee of quality to Parliament and the public and most of all to their own students. This part of the report, which suggests that the universities should themselves establish an academic review body, will not be easy for the universities, naturally proud of their independence, to welcome. But I think that they should do so — asking themselves:

5   Is the possession of a charter, and the system of external examiners, a sufficient guarantee of academic quality?

Let me add, as a footnote to this discussion, a word about the role of the validating universities. I am not one of those who would favour a monopoly role for any particular validator, and I value the diversity, variety and quality of validation provided by the group of validating universities. Nevertheless, I take the strict view that a validating university should insist that the standard of any degrees it gives its name to, whether internal or external or associated, should be the same, and should be seen to be the same, and should therefore bear the same title.

The funding of research in higher education is currently a major topic of debate. In addition to another of the Leverhulme volumes (*The Future of Research* edited by Geoffrey Oldham), summarized in the Leverhulme Report, there is also the recent NAB discussion document 'Research Policy in Local Authority Higher Education', and (most importantly) the report of the working party of the Advisory Board for the Research Councils (ABRC) on the support given by research councils for in-house and university research. A consensus is beginning to emerge which

(a)   defends the dual support system for funding university research, but
(b)   recognizes a role for applied research in major local authority institutions such as polytechnics, and
(c)   proposes that research funding should (both between institutions and within institutions) be *explicit, selective* and *ear-marked*.

According to this model, institutions (which did not already have them) would need to set up research committees to distribute selectively the separately-identified research funds, and to monitor the outcome. And funding bodies (the University Grants Committee and the National Advisory Body) would be required to identify the level of research support given to each institution, explain the grounds of selectivity, and review the results. The most important change proposed, however, would be the clear separation of the teaching and research functions, and the separate funding of each. Recent work by the DES on intersectoral comparisons of funding takes a step in that direction when it suggests that some 25% of UGC funds are to be considered as allocated for research. This part of the report (and the wider debate of recent months) suggests the following question:

6 Are all universities, and all departments in universities, to be funded for research by the UGC and (conversely) are no polytechnics (or departments within polytechnics) to be funded for research by NAB?

The section of the Leverhulme Report on the academic profession contains a number of important suggestions, and is worth careful study. But, undoubtedly its most important and contentious proposal is on the subject of tenure. 'There is a strong case for treating university teachers like their research and public sector colleagues and protecting their rights through employment protection legislation (which did not exist until relatively recently) rather than seeking to maintain lifetime tenure as the standard form of university appointment' (p.18). The arguments for such a view are cogently set out in detail in the Leverhulme volume *Response to Adversity* (Williams and Blackstone 1983). One reason why I would not wish to defend tenure is because I doubt whether an institution which practises it can be truly free or properly responsible. And I would like to maximize institutional freedom and responsibility. Let me ask one question on the subject:

7 Is it to be recommended that the university system of tenure be extended to local authority higher education, which at present does not enjoy it?

The section of the report on the binary system is another where Bruce Williams introduces a note of dissent. All signatories are agreed upon the main theme of the report: the endorsement of diversity, but while Sir Bruce thinks that a clearly-defined multi-sector system will best protect and promote diversity, the rest of the signatories recognize without concern the gradual blurring of the binary line. Indeed what has been said, for example, about the need to guarantee academic quality or about the funding of research, contributes to such a blurring. The creation of NAB, the decision of the voluntary colleges to come within its scope, and the developing relations and links between NAB and the UGC, all help towards the creation of a single but plural system, where diversity would be a characteristic more of institutions, not so much of sectors. It will be interesting to see whether that process continues, or is arrested by government.

The tenth section of the report deals with the role of government. There is first a discussion of local authority ownership of polytechnics and colleges and a difficult balance is drawn between the need and wish to maintain the role of the local authorities and the desire to protect and (indeed) increase institutional freedom. This is followed by a discussion of the relations between the UGC and NAB, the two major funding bodies in British higher education. The signatories propose that the two bodies should agree common funding criteria for the many activities that are common to the two sectors. The DES work on intersectoral comparisons, under consideration by NAB, and the subject of discussions with the UGC, is a contribution towards agreed funding criteria, but final agreement and common practice will not be easily achieved. The essential question is:

8 Should institutions (on either side of the binary line) receive the same money for the same work? (And if not, why not?)

The final major section of the report deals with the institutions and their funding. It is proposed (p.27) that each institution (university, polytechnic or college) should have an academic development plan recognized by its main funding body as being consistent with broad national and regional policies. It is suggested that each institution should receive four types of funds – core funding from the appropriate major funding body – programme funding for specific teaching programmes and research projects (which might come from a variety of resources) – fees from students who had exercised their choice of institution – and earned income through the commissioning (by, for example, industry or local government) of full-cost courses or applied research. This approach to funding would represent a major departure from present arrangements. NAB is at present considering some of its components: our Industry Group is discussing core and programme funding, and we are also giving thought to providing institutions with the freedom and incentive to earn outside income.

I have observed that the main theme of the Leverhulme Report is an endorsement of diversity – and I would certainly expect it to receive a diverse response. The central issue at the heart of the report is the conflict between central planning and a market-controlled system: my last question is on that subject:

9   Will we be better served by a system that is market controlled, or one that is centrally planned, or is the balanced approach to be favoured that is recommended by the Leverhulme Report?

The report does not offer a blueprint for the future; rather it sets the agenda for the debate. I do not believe that the issues it raises will go away, or can be ignored. NAB has begun to discuss (in some way or another) almost every one of the proposals, sometimes having anticipated them, sometimes learning from the report; several of the important issues are to be found in the NAB discussion document which is at present under consideration in local authority higher education. We expect to receive, and in turn to give, firm answers to the questions raised by Leverhulme.

Will the universities do likewise?

12

Freedom and Responsibility

The arguments drawn from the Leverhulme Report that were presented in the previous chapter were largely restated at the 1983 annual residential meeting of the Open University in September in Milton Keynes — where I addressed the Council on the subject of institutional freedom and responsibility. I also made — yet another — attempt to define the agenda for a debate about the future of higher education. But a major new point arose, in a concluding discussion of the roles of the central bodies (planning, funding, quality assurance) and the legitimate and essential freedoms and responsibilities of individual institutions. Although I had expected this to cause some controversy, it didn't. And in due course (and with some adjustment) the ideas outlined here found their way into the National Advisory Body's strategic advice to the Secretary of State in 1984.

Developments like the creation of the National Advisory Body (or, in the field of non-advanced further education, the establishment of the Manpower Services Commission) constitute a marked strengthening of central planning in higher education. Further evidence of this trend can be seen in the Secretary of State's letters to the University Grants Committee dated 14 July 1982, to the National Advisory Body dated 21 February 1983, and most recently to the UGC again, dated 1 September 1983. The growing resolution of government to encourage and facilitate a more effective central planning of higher education is not, in my view, to be regretted. On balance, I think it should be welcomed, but perhaps I should leave it to others to judge whether the strengthening of the central planning function in higher education is desirable, and will prove to be beneficial. What I am sure about is that it will only be so if it is counter-poised by a carefully-restated and vigorously-defended doctrine of institutional freedom and (the other side of the same coin) institutional responsibility. Section XI of the Leverhulme Report, *Excellence in Diversity*, has this to say about the institutions of higher education: '...Any external intervention between student and teacher, or between scholar and scholarship, needs to be justified.... Universities, colleges and polytechnics are the basic administrative units responsible for allocating resources. They should have the maximum possible discretion in managing their own affairs....' My main thesis is that, as we face the difficult problems and difficult years ahead of us, we must ensure that the growing strength of central planning is paralleled and met by a redefinition and reassertion of institutional freedom and responsibility. This is not a new thought: on the first day of NAB's existence, on 1 February 1982, a press notice was issued containing the following sentence: 'Perhaps the major challenge faced by the NAB will be to solve problems of the appropriate balance between national, regional and local planning in higher education and the legitimate and necessary freedom of institutions to develop in their own way.'

That still constitutes a challenge today, both for those concerned with central planning (at the UGC or NAB) and for each individual institution in higher education. As the providing bodies (local and central government) and the institutions come to grips with it, the appropriate balance must be defined and maintained between institutional freedom and responsibility, on the one hand, and central control and direction, on the other. The existence of university charters appears to raise the question why there should be central control and direction at all. The answer is that the public has a right to expect government (the providing bodies and their advisors) to give assurances about *funding* and *planning*, and to see that assurances are given about *quality* — that the funds are well spent, that the courses meet the nation's needs, and that the academic standards are satisfactory. In the university system the provision for these assurances is at present somewhat defective; the UGC is answerable for funding but can only plan the academic provision by means of exhortation and the crude instrument of financial control. Quality, if in question, is monitored by the (inadequate) system of external examiners.

In the local authority sector, since the 'capping of the pool' and the creation of NAB, an adequate system of central control is being developed for funding, for planning (where the present 'course approvals' mechanism is probably too strong a device), and for quality (where the validators and HM Inspectorate, together with external examiners, provide a powerful assurance). The concern in this sector is not how to strengthen the central powers, but rather how to establish and maintain an appropriate degree of institutional freedom and responsibility.

For the institutions, whether local authority or university or others, to play their full part in maintaining this essential balance between central direction and control (on the one hand) and institutional freedom and responsibility (on the other) we must ensure an adequate measure of decentralization and institutional independence. It is not fair to criticize institutions for failure to achieve responsible planning in circumstances in which they are deprived of the freedom and independence to do so. And it is the duty, as much of the institutions of higher education as of the central bodies such as NAB or UGC, to define that essential measure of freedom. As a young man, when I was fellow of Lincoln College, Oxford, about twenty years ago, I thought these questions were easy to answer. I remember we told Lord Franks' Commission on the University of Oxford that the essential independence of the college could be summarized as freedom to select our own undergraduates, freedom to appoint our own tutors, freedom to spend our own endowments, within the provisions of the College Statutes. Even in those days, we recognized the legitimate and limiting authority of one central body (the Privy Council) over the fullest expression of academic freedom. Nowadays, matters are not so simple, and we all recognize the legitimate and limiting authority of central bodies over institutions of higher education in the realms of planning and funding — and (I suggest) we should also do so in the realm of assurance of quality — validation. Within such a framework the essential freedoms and responsibilities of the institution need to be redefined, restated and protected. What might they look like?

The first essential is the freedom and responsibility to draw up academic plans (both for teaching and research), to discuss them with the appropriate central body, and (once approved) to implement them and bring them to successful fruition (or, alternatively, to fail and take the consequences). Although it seems unlikely that the quinquennial system can be readily reintroduced, we must try to ensure the integrity of 3-year planning and funding horizons if the institutions are to undertake their role responsibly.

The second is the freedom and responsibility to spend one's own budget, once it has been agreed with the providing body. I believe, for example, that the major institutions in local authority higher education should be left entirely free to choose how to spend the money allocated from the advanced further education pool provided that it is in accordance with the Secretary of State's decisions following advice from NAB. A polytechnic director has written to me that 'All we need is an approved budget and the freedom to spend it responsibly.' The last word is the key: responsible in whose eyes? *Freedom* will mean that it is the institution's governing body that decides what is responsible and what not. I have argued elsewhere that the time may have come — as the Leverhulme Report believes — for institutions with charters (that is, the universities) to consider establishing an academic review body to qualify their freedom under the charter to be the sole guarantee of academic quality. For major institutions without charters the time may have to come to consider the provision of corporate status, and hence (particularly) both the freedom and responsibility to act as their own employers, and the opportunity to plan their finance across the financial year end. Responsibility for acting as employers is responsibility for what the Americans call 'hiring and firing'. And at least two difficult points arise here: first, the inevitable problem responsible employers have in facing demands for staff pay increases (whether academic or non-academic) in excess of the funds available; and secondly, the question of lifetime tenure. The Leverhulme Report is strongly in favour of protecting university teachers' rights through today's employment protection legislation rather than by giving appointments for life. One overriding reason why I would not wish to defend tenure is because I doubt whether an institution which practises it can be truly free or properly responsible.

It is, of course, the task of the institutions themselves to redefine the freedoms that they need and the responsibilities they are prepared to undertake. I hope they will do so. But whether we talk of institutional freedom, or academic freedom, or any other sort of freedom, I am certain of one thing: freedom and responsibility are inseparable partners.

13

Doomsday – or the Responsive Model?

The National Advisory Body's first major planning exercise was completed by December 1983, and it became clear that we were able to fulfil our terms of reference. At the annual conference of the Society for Research into Higher Education in Loughborough I spoke after dinner on the future of higher education. Unfortunately – or perhaps, not – the jokes have been mislaid: what remains is a heartfelt plea to my colleagues in higher education to break out of the defensive stance and offer a more positive response to the nation's educational needs. 'Higher education', I said, 'is responsible for its own future... resources usually follow coherent purpose.'

The future for higher education sometimes appears to offer little more than a fierce and unequal struggle between the government and the defenders of higher education for adequate resources, though I personally believe that its future will be more complicated, more interesting and more purposeful than that.

Higher education is in some ways less than true to itself in its attachment to traditional forms and methods, and in its apparent suspicion of innovation and new ideas. Tradition can be fruitful ground for inspiration and renewal, an anchor, a force for unity and continuity, but it can also be moribund. Suspicion and defensiveness will inevitably be counter-productive. We are entering an era of considerable change in British higher education and it will surely be better for the nation if the changes are largely created and carried through by the initiative of institutions and teachers rather than by fiat of government or planning bodies. How can a planning body like ours, the National Advisory Body, liberate initiative, encourage responsibility and develop confidence at the institutional level and within institutions? This is no idle rhetorical question but a central one which we must seek to answer in the next few years.

In considering the next decade it might be fruitful to look at two possible and contrasting models for British higher education – the 'doomsday' and the 'responsive' models. Briefly, the 'doomsday' model assumes that there will be no serious attempt on the part of central and local planners to extend access to higher education by meeting the needs of adult and continuing education or of non-traditional entrants. It assumes the maintenance of a high threshold of entry defined in terms of, traditionally, A level scores and the continuation of specialized 3-year degree courses as the norm. It also assumes a 20% reduction in the level of qualified and willing 18-year-old entrants to higher education, together with a reduction in the unit of resource for the whole system in the order of, let us say, a further 10%. Within this model there may be perhaps 100 major institutions (50 university institutions and 50 polytechnics and major colleges) and an even-handed reduction on both sides of the binary line. But will there be an even-handed approach, an even-handed reduction of resources on either side of the binary line? Anything other than even-handedness will surely create an insoluble management problem for the 'disadvantaged' sector, be it the universities or the public sector. The case for integrated planning, to meet the longer-term needs of our society, is surely self-evident.

On the other hand, the so called 'responsive' model assumes (in line with the Leverhulme Report) a serious and early attempt by all sectors of higher education to explore the new markets within the adult and continuing education field and among the non-traditional entrants to higher education. Hand in hand with this, there must be a willingness to consider the evidence of stagnation in participation in the 1970s, and a willingness to re-design courses and entrance requirements, to review course lengths, to consider cost-effectiveness at the points in the system which affect student support and research funding, and to develop a working partnership with government and industry to offer a service to the nation that can be shown to be effective. Access to higher education must no longer be defined in terms of the Robbins principle: it is an inadequate formulation for the future. We must explore the limits of participation which will be useful and profitable to society and rewarding for the individual. I do not believe that we are yet near the margins. This model assumes that if access is as flexible as policy-makers and institutions can allow so too will be the funding for higher education. It is my firm belief that resources usually follow coherent and well argued purpose. I see this as the major challenge for the system over the next ten years: to create the 'responsive' or the 'doomsday' model. It is as much the choice of those of us who are working within the higher education system as it is of government.

Higher education is responsible for its own future. I hope that local authority institutions and voluntary colleges will join together with NAB to realize something like the responsive model. If this is to be done, it will be by defining and defending the distinctive contribution of the public sector of higher education and by adhering to the principle of adapting institutions where necessary to achieve 'fitness for purpose'. I expect NAB to continue to boost the importance of part-time students (and of adult and continuing education in general), and of non-degree work, and to plan for a system of dispersed access to higher education built around a range of major institutions of proven quality without neglect to the needs of full-time students and of degree-level work. I believe this will be achieved by the use of a selective approach incorporating the twin criteria of quality and economy. I do not believe that the nation will willingly or lightly dismantle and throw away a system of higher education that can and has proved itself to be cost-effective, and of quality, which is striving to meet the needs of employers, and is offering opportunities to a wide range of students including the non-traditional groups, the unemployed, late developers and other mature students, adults requiring professional updating or retraining, and those who live far away from the nearest university.

Disraeli, who believed that 'upon the education of the people of this country the fate of this country depends', also said that 'change is inevitable: in a progressive country change is constant.' British higher education must learn not just not to resist change, not just to permit it, but to volunteer and create change; I believe that the system *is* capable of taking the initiative, in order to confront the difficult years ahead, and I hope that it will do so creatively and with purpose.

14

The Eighth Principle

Back to Sheffield. Eighteen months after the CLEA conference (see Chapter 6), the North of England Education Conference also met there, at the beginning of 1984, and my subject was the future of public sector higher education. The slight shift of emphasis from local authority to public sector higher education (later to be adopted in the title of the reconstituted National Advisory Body) reflected the courageous decision of the voluntary colleges taken at the end of 1983 to place themselves within the scope of NAB. This paper gives some emphasis to the growing feeling that the Robbins principle of access required redefinition — and also to the role of the awards regulations as the 'hidden hand' in British higher education policy. Before 1984 was ended these topics had become national issues and together they represent, I believe, the major challenge to those responsible for higher education in 1985.

Seven principles seem to me to characterize the distinctive importance of the local authority sector of higher education and provide a reasonable and defensible basis upon which future work should be founded, both in the short and in the longer term. They have stood up well to the test of time — by which I mean more than the last year and a half. They were not new when I first listed them (see Chapter 6), and they will outlast my involvement in higher education:

1 The local and regional emphasis of local authority higher education.
2 The fruitful co-existence of advanced and non-advanced further education — the mixture of levels.
3 The mixture of modes — the co-existence of full-time, sandwich and part-time work.
4 The primacy of teaching.
5 Cost-effectiveness.
6 Responsiveness to need — whether expressed by student demand, or the requirements of employment, or the policies of local or national government.
7 Concern for quality, guaranteed by threshold validation and HM Inspectorate.

The work of the National Advisory Body has from the start been firmly grounded on these seven principles. They have not been seriously challenged: they have not been added to — though I now propose that there is an eighth.

Public sector higher education is plannable. While the University Grants Committee and the universities wrestle with their own peculiar problems — an indiscriminate (or insufficiently discriminate) system of research funding, for example, or the lack of an adequate external peer-review system, or the albatross of tenure, or the difficulty of achieving effective national planning without infringing the freedoms granted by university charters — while these and other complex questions confront the university sector, the public sector has for the first time proved itself responsive to national planning. This will, I believe, prove to be one of its greatest strengths in the future.

Setting aside for the moment the development of NAB's longer-term strategy for local authority higher education, based on responses to its consultative document issued last summer, and the preparation for the next major planning exercise, to be conducted between the autumn of 1984 and 1986, we have a full programme of work for the next twelve months. Two of the detailed facets of the 1984/85 plan have given rise to further examination of the issues. The debate about the advice to be offered in relation to courses in town and country planning has led the Committee to ask for a further report, and the issue of concentration will come before the Committee again when it considers the Board's recommendations on a number of detailed cases. Both these pieces of work are expected to give rise to advice in respect of 1985/86.

On a more general level, the Committee has authorized three specific studies during 1984:

1   A review of the provision of art and design courses, especially those (DATEC) validated by BTEC in time for advice to be given on their location, concentration, and continuation or otherwise in 1985.
2   A review of the future place in the public sector, advanced further education system of colleges engaged (or recently engaged) in teacher education, especially those now categorized as diversified teacher training colleges, to include both their teacher training provision and their other work.
3   A reconsideration of the categorization of institutions, with the aim of making it possible effectively to recognize the contribution made by the major providers of advanced further education.

Work already in progress in a number of the working groups is expected to come to fruition in 1984. Substantial reports are expected from the Continuing Education and Industry Groups, and both the transbinary groups (Agriculture and Architecture) are due to report before or during the summer: the Engineering Group also has a number of issues before it on which reports are expected. Work on the definition and use of programmes, and on the practical realization of a system of programme approvals, must also be carried forward.

While little progress was made in the development and implementation of a research policy in 1983, it is not an issue which can be neglected, and I expect the Board and Committee to return to this topic during 1984. Here is an opportunity, I suggest, to explore, in a limited experiment in the public sector, a policy of explicit, selective and identified research funding for institutions of proven achievement or measurable promise in research, especially applied research. I hope we shall receive the encouragement of the local authorities and the DES, and the co-operation of the Research Councils, in an enterprise which could – if it were successful – offer benefits to the whole of higher education.

All these issues relate to NAB's overall responsibility for planning; most of them will affect the Committee's advice for 1985/86, and all of them the further development of NAB's task. At the same time, its overriding concern for quality means that further co-operation with HM Inspectorate and the major validators will continue to be a focus of activity, and that the consideration of a formal basis for NAB visitations to colleges will attract a high priority.

During 1983, negotiations with the voluntary colleges have been brought to a successful conclusion, and with effect from November they have been formally incorporated within NAB's responsibilities. Although three new members of the Board representative of voluntary college interests have been appointed, much remains to be done. At the very least, the NAB database must be enlarged, and consequential matters of detail attended to. More significantly, the reviews referred to above (especially that of teacher education and diversified colleges) have taken on a new dimension. The Committee looks forward to the development of its responsibilities across the two sectors of higher education, and welcomes the voluntary college interests to the local government/central government partnership in NAB: it awaits the setting up of the Voluntary Sector Consultative Council with interest.

The two most substantial tasks of NAB in 1984, however, will be the development of a strategy for the late 1980s and beyond, and the preparation for the next major planning exercise. Responses to the long-term strategy document due to be sent to NAB by the end of 1983 will be reviewed during 1984, and the approach to the second major planning round will reflect the Committee's view of an appropriate strategy for the latter years of the decade. NAB hopes to co-operate with the University Grants Committee and others in advising the Secretary of State, in response to his request, on the directions in which higher education in the United Kingdom might move.

It would be wrong for me at this stage – before the responses have been read, considered and evaluated – to speculate too freely or too precisely, about the likely outcome of this national consultation on higher education strategy. But I expect, among many other important conclusions and proposals, two particular outcomes: a reconsideration and more precise redefinition of Robbins' first guiding principle of access to higher education, and a radical review of the DES awards regulations. Robbins stated: 'We have assumed as an axiom that courses of higher education should be available for all those who are qualified by ability and attainment to pursue them, and who wish to do so.' No harm in that: it provided a valuable touchstone for the 60s and 70s, when the expansion and provision for the 18-year-old student intake was the primary task, but it is an inadequate formulation for the rest of the century, a period when the needs of adult and continuing education will rank equally with those of the 18-year-old school-leaver. In particular, the two-A level test will need to be reconsidered and replaced. As for the awards regulations, there can be little doubt that the Leverhulme Report is right to say that 'present financial arrangements, particularly those for student grants, discourage institutions from offering, and students from seeking, courses other than those leading to full-time Honours degrees.' The role of the awards regulations as a sort of 'hidden hand' in British higher education policy must be, first, understood and then (if necessary) reconsidered.

The outcome of this consultative exercise – together with the UGC's similar inquiry – will provide the strategic underpinning to the next planning exercise, which will (I hope) be undertaken and completed with less haste than the first. This one will involve the submission of proposals by all colleges and authorities, will be timetabled over a somewhat more extended period starting in the early autumn of 1984, and will relate principally to the academic year 1987/88.

We have learned lessons from the operation of NAB's first short-term planning exercise. Apart from the need for an extended timetable, and for an agreed, approved and understood strategic framework for the next planning exercise, a third lesson I would draw from this year's experience is that not again can we afford in this country to plan one half of higher education in ignorance of – or without taking full and proper account of – the other half. The need for integrated planning of British higher education in future is evident. Indeed, the terms of reference of NAB point in that direction: the Committee is required, in formulating its advice, 'to contribute to *a co-ordinated approach to provision*, as necessary in relevant academic fields, between the local authority and the university, voluntary and direct grant sectors of higher education.' This, the fourth term of reference of the Committee (together with the third, on monitoring the implementation of dispositions made by the Secretary of State on NAB's advice) will provide the next major challenge to NAB and its partners.

How are we to achieve a co-ordinated approach to provision? There are two main difficulties: first, the geographical one – while the UGC is responsible for a UK system, NAB is for England only. If that problem is to be resolved, it will not be for NAB to do it; and, until it is tackled, we for our part shall be content to concentrate on working for a co-ordinated approach to provision in England. The second difficulty is sectoral: to build and strengthen the bridge between the UGC and NAB, and the links between the universities and the public sector at institutional, local, regional and national levels. Above all, we need an effective national forum where integrated planning can take place. The regular meetings between the Chairmen of the UGC and of the Boards of NAB and the Wales Advisory Body offer a promising start to the achievement of a co-ordinated approach to provision, but more must be done. The need for planning, and for integrated planning, is both evident and urgent.

15

There'll Never be a Better Year

For some reason (now forgotten) I was feeling particularly hopeful at the time when, in March 1984, I was asked to speak to the annual general meeting of the Association of Colleges of Further and Higher Education on strategies for higher education during the next ten years. The themes of the previous paper (Chapter 14) were further developed: in particular, I had come to believe — and still do — that 'the fundamental question is the question of access.' But access to what? What pattern of courses should we be planning to meet the needs of extended access? How are we to talk about the wide-ranging curriculum of modern higher education? Are all subjects either *arts* or *sciences*? Why do the disciplines appear to be such an incoherent jumble? The attempt here to provide an analysis and reclassification of the disciplines may be compared with the endeavour (in Chapter 18) to discuss transferable skills. This is difficult country, but those who propose to undertake educational planning must find pathways through it if they are to do their job properly.

The weather is right: the time is here
There'll never be a better year!
(Buffie Sainte-Marie)

1984 should be seen as the year of opportunity for higher education; the debate on the future of higher education, stimulated by the National Advisory Body discussion document and carried forward by the University Grants Committee questionnaire, provides a real challenge to all in higher education (the government included) to redefine and reassert our purpose, and gives a genuine opportunity to reform and redesign advanced further education (AFE) to meet the needs of the 1990s and beyond.

Over 150 responses were received to the NAB discussion document; at the time of writing they had not been fully analysed, but the central questions and concerns were clear. The fundamental one being, of course, the question of access. For how many students do we want to provide higher education? The Robbins Report gave a definitive answer: for all those who are qualified by ability and attainment and who wish to have it.

This definition served well enough for twenty years, but it will prove to be inadequate as a yardstick for the future (not because it goes too far, but because it does not — in practice — go far enough) — for three reasons. First, the achievements (especially of public sector higher education) have shown that the idea of the 'qualified student' must allow not only for qualification by examination and certificate but also (and with increasing importance) for qualification by experience. Secondly, the Robbins definition has led to concentration almost exclusively on the question of access for the 18+ school-leaver to full-time and sandwich courses and to a temptation to overlook the needs of mature students (including the unemployed) for adult and continuing education, often part-time — whether for updating, retraining or traditional liberal studies. And thirdly it suggests — wrongly — that there is a natural level of access to AFE, whereas access is in fact *managed*; whatever level of access is achieved is the intended (or unintended) result of various educational policies.

The argument for extending access to higher education is *not* to save institutions or to preserve jobs but rather to provide the level of qualified manpower the economy will need in the 1990s and beyond, and to develop a more generally educated society. It is one of the special tasks of public sector higher education to explore the limits of access and to see how far it is possible to extend opportunities for higher education without sacrificing the quality of the education offered while maintaining the provision of personal and social and economic benefits. The key to any adequate strategy for higher education for the next decade and beyond must surely be the extension of access, and some of the implications for the United Kingdom system and its management of such a policy are considered further in the following sections.

The first problem is that of *admissions* to higher education not that of adequate resources, which comes later. One of the most important reasons for seeking a more comprehensive and integrated system of admissions following the establishment of the Polytechnic Central Admissions Scheme by the Committee of Directors of Polytechnics is to provide a better assessment than we have at present of the 'real field' — the pool of qualified and willing candidates for full-time and sandwich courses. The higher education system of the future, however, whatever its size and shape, must also provide for dispersed access. Not all students are mobile. Mature students and part-time students typically need access to local institutions: and it is probably true that the non-traditional entrant is often more readily attracted to a local college than to a more distant institution. If we are serious about the extension of access, we must provide a system that meets the needs of such students. It is for this reason that NAB has insisted upon a regional approach: and it is for this reason that the issue of concentration of provision upon large institutions is so difficult. Those who urge the importance of dispersed access to higher education are right but so are those who wish to strengthen the major institutions; they can and should come together to plan for a system of access to higher education built round a range of major institutions of proven quality.

In order to develop a common system the whole of higher education and not only the public sector must come under review. Some institutions (many of the universities and some of the polytechnics — in some cases, parts of them only) have chosen for themselves a predominantly national — or even international – role, and where that can be properly sustained, it should be respected. Most institutions however cannot and should not (and indeed do not wish to) aspire to a predominantly national role. The importance of the principle of dispersed access cannot be overstressed, and certain institutions (of all kinds) have a vital strategic role to play in its development.

It has become apparent that if our aim is the extension of access then integrated planning of United Kingdom higher education is essential: colleges, polytechnics and universities in each of the sectors and all of the parts of the United Kingdom must be considered together. That is a task for government to tackle in the first instance. However, NAB intends to offer advice in its next planning exercise (for 1987/88) – so far as the provision for which it is responsible is concerned – in the context of an overview of the totality of higher education, arrived at in co-operation with the UGC and the Wales Advisory Body. A second task – equally important – is to recognize that the borderline between NAFE and AFE is an arbitrary one and somewhat blurred, and that integrated planning is required between them too. Here NAB (together with its partners in the regional advisory councils and with the Manpower Services Commission) can play a leading role in co-operative planning with the local education authorities.

The current awards regulations – and the pattern of student support – are a sort of 'hidden hand' in British higher education policy. It is important that, as part of his strategic review, the Secretary of State should not omit a review of the existing regulations, and consider their effect on provision. We need to question – not for the first time – the rigidity of the 3 (or 4)-year mandatory awards system; the possibility of separating fee-support from grant; and the parental means-test. A system of 2-year mandatory grants, with the right to fees for the third year, is surely worth considering in the interests of extending access. On this pattern, some students might choose to leave higher education for employment after two years and complete their third year later (and it would be important to allow such students to take *2 further years of part-time* fees, instead of *1 year full-time* if they wished). Others would complete a 3-year course by supporting themselves for the third year, whereas some would find a 2-year course sufficient for their requirements. Where manpower needs operate most clearly, for example in medicine or initial teacher training, longer grants could be made available. Such a system, which offers more control to the student-customer (consumer) would provide a more effective planning mechanism than today's inevitably crude central planning. The needs of adult and continuing education, similarly, will be best met if the potential student is offered his or her fees to spend on the course best fitted to his or her needs. Such a scheme, far from suggesting the abolition of fees, uses the mechanism of fee-support as a key to ensuring the responsiveness of institutions and courses to perceived need.

What pattern of courses will meet the needs of extended access? C.P. Snow's essay on 'The Two Cultures' does more harm than good, if it is understood to offer a binary split of education into 'arts' and 'science'. Similarly, the commonplace contrast between 'education' and 'training' suggests an analysis of learning that is justified neither by theory, commonsense nor experience. One is uneasy with both the heavy (but unspecified) moral freight carried by the term 'education' and the narrow instrumentalism of 'training'. And both terms suggest that students are 'practised upon' by their teachers (or trainers). *Learning* is a more neutral term for the activity in which we are all engaged – students and teachers alike.

Peter Scott has written: 'It has become difficult to talk about the basic purposes of the university (he might have said 'of higher education' or – indeed – 'of education generally') in a way that is both intelligible and respectable'; 'Disciplinary and professional specialization has decisively shifted the territory of the modern university away from the broader educational and intellectual considerations that must be an important ingredient in any debate about its future which tries to be both wide-ranging and fundamental.... As a result higher education policy itself has become entirely divorced from public culture.'

This is a just criticism, and a challenge to all of us concerned with higher education. How are we to discuss what we are doing in language that is neither esoteric nor over-simplified? How are we to talk about subjects, or disciplines, without, on the one hand, involving the simplistic and misleading opposition of arts and science or, on the other hand, resorting to the complexities of the DES (list 209) subject codes, the UCG's (37) subject areas or NAB's (14) programmes?

One possible approach would be to develop four broad categories: The *explanatory sciences* (mathematics, physics, chemistry, for example), the *effective sciences* (engineering, technology, design, for example), the *service disciplines* (education, law, librarianship, for example) and the *value disciplines* (history, English, fine art, philosophy, sociology, for example). One difficulty is that many subjects (perhaps most) seem to belong to two or more categories; yet the idea of a fourfold division of the curriculum is not altogether useless if it draws attention to some of the central questions of education – Explanation: how does it work? Effectiveness: how can I make it work? Service: how can I help? Value: what is worthy and what is excellent? Although one or other of these issues will predominate in any subject, most good courses raise – in differing proportions – all four of them.

We live in an intellectual era, part of a long period within the history of ideas, where the concepts and methods of the explanatory sciences have so dominated higher education and advanced thought that they have begun to crowd out, and do damage to, the effective sciences and the disciplines of service and of value. A sound educational system should strive to maintain the balance between these four categories. Furthermore, the explanatory sciences, which have prospered so remarkably through the application of experimental research methods, have led us to embrace twin heresies: that higher education is characteristically research-related; and that higher education is *essentially* specialized; neither is (or should be) true. It may be true that progress in the explanatory sciences depends on the specialized, research-related education of *some* of the very ablest of each generation. It is not true that a sound education for every student of the explanatory sciences, or for students of the effective sciences, and the service and value disciplines, depends on the provision of specialized research-related courses. It is not the sole or even the primary function of higher education to produce 'dons', to supply the next generation of teachers.

What is the special and distinctive role of the public sector in the higher education strategy for the future? In one sense there is no particular role for any sector – rather institutions (colleges, polytechnics and universities) must each define their own distinctive and appropriate roles; diversity of institutions is valuable, and should be maintained. Nevertheless, we should look to the existing public sector institutions to take particular care to provide for part-time and sandwich work, as well as full-time work; for degree equivalent and sub-degree work, as well as degree-level work; for what I have termed the effective sciences and the service disciplines, as well as for the explanatory sciences and the value disciplines; and (above all) for regional and local demand in safeguarding opportunities for dispersed access to higher education, and providing for local and regional employment needs.

The fundamental question for higher education in the future must be that of access; we must determine upon, plan for and invest in access. The most recent statement from the government is, therefore, not unencouraging: 'The Government's main objectives for Higher Education are to maintain access for all those who want it and are suitably qualified, to improve efficiency and learning in all sectors whilst maintaining standards, to secure a further shift in provision towards science, engineering and technology, where the output of graduates is set to increase, and to maintain the quantity and quality of research' (Government Expenditure Plans 1984).

Keble College, my college in Oxford, was founded in 1870 to provide for (I quote) 'young men now debarred from University education'. A little more than a century later we in the public sector must carry forward that work and provide for many – not only the young, not only the men – who are at present unable to achieve higher education.

There'll never be a better year!...

And the song continues:

> It's time to plant a brand-new world
> Where promises keep and paths unfurl
> To young and old, to boy and girl,
> To rich and poor, to woman and man,
> To black and white and gold and tan
> To big and little and fast and slow,
> O see how brotherhood can grow!...
> The weather is right: the time is here.
> There'll never be a better year!...

That's my vision. What is yours?

16

Defective Partnership – or Triple Alliance?

This paper, and the next (Chapter 17), were delivered at the Careers Research and Advisory Centre conferences in Cambridge in March and April 1984. I hoped to achieve three things by the account I gave at the first meeting of the relationship between industry and higher education. First of all, there seemed to be a need for exposition – for describing what public sector higher education was doing, and how the National Advisory Body was tackling the issue of this 'defective partnership'. Secondly, I wanted to attempt an analysis of some underlying and abiding problems, such as academic drift or the pressure of uninformed student demand. Thirdly and most importantly, I wished to add my voice to those who were calling for a renewed and effective triple alliance – of the world of employment, government and the educational service. A year or so later, and with the reports of the Butcher Committee on information technology manpower before me, I perceive an uncertain response. We still need a clear signal from each of the partners. Those of us in education have spoken out. What does industry think? What has government to say?

I regret what I perceive as a defective partnership between institutions of higher education and the wealth-producing sectors of the community on the one hand, and government on the other. It is a dialogue of the deaf – or (at least) the hard of hearing. From government we seem to hear too much about economy and efficiency (those inadequate or ill-defined virtues) and too little of the purposes and values of education. From the world of employment come precise messages about short-term needs – too often too late for a satisfactory response from higher education (with its long lead-times) – and imprecise, undecipherable, blurred messages about the longer term which leave us puzzled and frustrated. And the responses from higher education all too frequently strike the auditors as little more than a claim for more resources with less interference. Each perceives, and purveys, a caricature of the other. A defective partnership, and an ill-served nation.

If we are to convert this defective partnership into an effective triple alliance (of the world of employment, government, and the education service), we must clearly recognize, and respect, some of the critically difficult issues that face us. First, *timescale* – the conflict between the immediacy of identified employment needs and the relatively long lead-times for planning, implementation and completion in higher education; second *need or demand* – the tension between manpower planning and responsiveness to informed student demand; third, *representation* – the question of whether the employers' contribution to higher education can most effectively be made through central planning bodies (like NAB), or on governing bodies, or (as I believe) at course or departmental level; fourth, *resources* – the undeniable need for adequate resources, intelligently delivered (whether through institutional funding or student awards) so as to promote and enhance an effective partnership between higher education and industry; fifth, *morale* – a high order of leadership is required to rebuild morale – to liberate initiative, encourage responsibility and develop confidence in the triple alliance of industry, government and education.

Perhaps the most important – and intractable – of these is the question of *need or demand*. How are we to reconcile the approach to the planning of higher education which tries to provide the required skilled manpower for specific employment needs (as in medicine or education, at present) with the alternative model which – following the Robbins Report – bases forward planning on informed student demand? The difficulties – particularly – of providing the right mix of subjects and of levels of study is well known, and my own doubts and caution in trying to do too much by centralized manpower planning to meet specific vocational needs are longstanding. There is of course a need and a place for a large number of specific vocational courses, but they should be designed – and often redesigned from time to time – in close consultation with the relevant employers. And that is a task for institutions and departments, not for central planners at the National Advisory Body or the University Grants Committee, though they need to be satisfied that the job is being done. Moreover it is not clear that in the realms of general education employers necessarily or always want a high level of expertise in science or technology; often they seem to be looking more for holders of final qualifications who are generally well educated, and, while claiming no expertise, are not frightened by quantitative methods or unacquainted with scientific or technological principles. It is general vocational relevance, not specific vocational skills, that we should be especially concerned to provide in courses. Content is not all: the socialization (and sorting) functions of education must not be overlooked. Competence in communication, teamwork and problem solving are highly valued transferable skills, important both to the individual and to the employers. And a higher education system which achieves a balance between what I have elsewhere called the explanatory and effective sciences and the service and value disciplines (Chapter 15), will be better able to provide these than one which is abruptly and excessively redirected by central planners who, failing to respect the pattern of informed student demand, insist instead on a decisive shift towards science and technology, and vocational courses.

The Industry Group of NAB, in offering advice on the 1984/85 planning exercise, indicated its own scepticism on this point. Yet some decision has to be made about the broad division between subject areas. As is well known, a decision to do nothing is in effect a planning decision.

NAB decided to favour the scientific, technological and business studies areas in providing student places in institutions in 1984/85, and to promote a measured shift of the system in that direction. I have read of concerns that there will be shortages in key engineering and computing skills in a few years' time because of recent university cutbacks. Well, in the local authority sector, we have provided for an extra 15% first-year full-time students in engineering in 1984 compared with 1982, and an impressive 47% increase in maths and computing full-time students over the same period.

My concern, if I have one, is not whether we have provided sufficient places in these areas, but whether sufficient students of the right calibre will come forward to fill them. A planning organization is primarily concerned with supply. It shares with others the responsibility for influencing demand, notably with government and industry. If we have too few of our most able people qualified in scientific and technological subjects (and I note the doubts of some about that assumption) how can we change the situation? Not just by providing more places. For if they are not taken up we must ask why. Is it a schooling problem? Possibly. I suspect, however, that more of the answer about student demand lies with the world of employment than with the world of education. NAB has provided the places for institutions to educate our future graduate and technician engineers and computing specialists. What is the world of employment doing to ensure that our students wish to obtain these qualifications? What are the relative salaries and prestige within companies (and indeed within our society) of the engineer and the marketing or finance man or woman? Answer that question and we may go a long way towards explaining the subject preferences of our students, who are not fools.

If (as I believe) the main engine in the planning of higher education should be *informed student demand*, there is a heavy responsibility resting upon each of the partners in the triple alliance (government, the employers, and the education service) to ensure that students are properly and thoroughly informed of the employment prospects relating to different subjects and courses. Here, I am quite sure, there is more to be done. Uninformed student demand is no safe basis for planning.

What about level? In its longer-term strategy document, NAB raised the question of degree versus diploma courses and 3- versus 2-year degrees. The responses would seem to indicate a suspicion of (or if you prefer, opposition to) a 2-year degree, but a more ready welcome to more 2-year courses at diploma level. Our industrialists on both the Industry and Engineering Groups tell us that we have too many graduates compared to technicians, that some students who took degree courses should have taken technician courses and are in reality employed as technicians. The Engineering Council's recent report on standards and routes to registration also raises the issue of recognizing the legitimate status of the technician route and not regarding it as a repository for mediocre graduates.

This is one area where advice seems to be consistent, and yet the prestige of graduate status is as well known as is the seemingly inexorable pressure to upgrade courses. If there is to be a shift in balance towards the 2-year technician level courses, towards the BTEC higher diplomas and away from the 3-year (specialized) Honours degree, how can it be done?

It is not easy to resist academic drift. Exhortation, by itself, has little effect;

more can be done by decisive planning by such bodies as NAB — seconded and supported by clear and unambiguous signals from partners in government and industry. But, to be really effective, we need first to understand (and, then, if necessary to reform) those features of the higher education system which combine to create the pressure towards academic drift. They are several, but they certainly include: (a) the prestige of the university system (which largely avoids sub-degree work), (b) the Burnham salary rules, (c) the current awards regulations, and (d) the desire of many professional bodies to upgrade qualifying courses to degree level to enhance the status of their professions.

Turning to the future, what kind of a higher education system do we want to see ten years from now? Higher education planning has become dominated, if not obsessed, by the future demographic decline associated with the low birthrate in the middle 70s. The results of that decline in terms of fewer students in higher education has been discussed almost exclusively in terms of its impact on the higher education system. But what about its effects on the economy? If there are 15 — 20% less students coming in, there will be 15 — 20% less coming out. Will industry and other employers — and government — be happy with a smaller pool of qualifed manpower? — at all levels not just at degree level. I suspect not. We ought to turn our attention to this aspect of the future demographic decline. Our country will need to develop all the talents available in its people to the greatest possible extent. The case for access and greater mature student entry will not rest just on the principle of wider opportunity, but on the real and pressing needs of our economy.

Some people see the approaching demographic decline as an impending disaster for higher education: others (and I am one of these) see a wonderful opportunity for extending access to advanced further education for part-time students, non-mobile students, and mature and non-traditional entrants (including the unemployed), and the possibility of creating a more generally educated society. But all must agree that, unless great care is taken, we shall certainly encounter a problem of shortfall of qualified manpower in ten years' time. Privately, many employers have told me that they would like to see a more educated workforce. NAB's Industry Group has said the same thing. Now is the time to say so publicly and loudly. We can no longer afford the defective partnership of which I have spoken — we never could afford it! The triple alliance of employment, government and the education service must, wthout delay, come together and co-operate to plan — not for the short-term — but for the longer-term development of a more educated workforce and a satisfactory supply of qualified manpower. We need a clear signal from each of the partners. Those of us in education have spoken out. What does industry think? What has government to say?

17

A Proper General Education

At the second CRAC conference (see Chapter 16 for the first) I was asked to speak about recent developments in higher education and their implications for student admissions. Oxford University (led by Keble) had recently decided to reform its admissions procedures: the Universities Central Council for Admissions had also agreed to develop, in partnership with the Committee of Directors of Polytechnics, the Polytechnic Central Admissions Scheme. These seemed to me significant advances – and they still do. But I wanted to look beyond the immediate concerns of admissions officers to the possibility of a truly comprehensive and integrated system of admissions to (full-time and sandwich) higher education. Without some such system we shall always be guessing at the 'real field' – the true level of demand from those who are able to benefit from higher education and who wish to do so. But there is a more important issue. Just as the student awards regulations are the 'hidden hand' of higher education planning, so also do our admissions arrangements determine more than just who studies where: they partly condition both the nature of our courses and the shape of sixth-form education. Admissions officers rule – but is it OK?

The object of our present discussion is to arrive at a satisfactory entrance qualification for universities, which may supersede the multiplicity of examinations now existing. It seems to me that one wants an examination which will fit in with the ordinary school curriculum, so that a boy can take it without having to prepare specially for it. It will merely show that he has had what we regard as a proper general education, and has reached a sufficient standard in it to justify his going on to a University... our object is to reduce the amount of *specialized* knowledge required.... I want to make it worth his while to keep up his other subjects to some considerable extent up to the end of his school career. I think our conversations with our scientific friends have a value apart from the conclusions at which we arrive. ... The subject is difficult enough, and the more wisdom we can have brought into the common stock the better.

These are the words of Frederick George Kenyon, Director and Principal Librarian of the British Museum, in a letter to T.F. Tout, Professor of

History at the University of Manchester, in 1918. Dr Peter Slee, a historian of higher education, currently at Manchester University, who kindly drew my attention to the letter, pertinently asked: 'What went wrong?'

Two-thirds of a century later, after countless inquiries, proposals, counter-proposals and reports — of which the two most notable, perhaps, the Robbins Report of 1963 and the Leverhulme Report of 1983, duly gave their support to the principle of what Kenyon called 'proper general education' — we find ourselves engaged in a national debate, at the heart of which lie three closely-related issues:

a the need for a broadening of sixth-form studies — Kenyon's hope for 'a proper general education' in schools;

b the admissions requirements of our universities, polytechnics and colleges of higher education; and

c the appropriate balance, within higher education, between general courses and more specifically vocational ones and (the third alternative — and a highly valued one) specialized, academic, research-related Honours courses.

Since at least 1918, those responsible for English education — it is not a Scottish problem — have struggled unavailingly to untie this intricate knot of issues. Perhaps a Secretary of State will come, like a modern Alexander, to put his sword to it: we shall see.

The pernicious mechanism, the vicious circle, is clear enough. And like most bad things, it grows in good soil. Our highly-valued, specialized, academic, research-related honours courses — typical of the university system, but also found in polytechnics — (together with the more specific vocational courses) impose a narrowing effect on admissions requirements, and lead to an overvaluing of the grades in the required three A levels and a consequential undervaluing of the rest of the school education. And this in turn defeats the good intentions of those who wish to see a broadening of sixth-form studies. The conflict between the defence of our research-ethos in higher education and our desire for Kenyon's 'proper general education' in schools, and indeed in a substantial part of higher education itself, must be clearly recognized. We cannot (apparently) have it both ways, and must choose. I believe this is one of the critical educational issues of our time, and I look for the day when we will finally recognize that specialized, research-related higher education is suitable for only a proportion of our young people and when such courses can be confined to a limited number of research universities. When that happens — before it can happen — we must learn to value equally with the high-prestige research-related courses the other two models: specific vocational courses, and general courses. Otherwise, future attempts at reform will fail like those that have gone before. In its response to the University Grants Committee's '28 questions', my own university expresses the problem as follows:

Our preference therefore would in principle be for such a broadening to be universally adopted, but we recognize the difficulty of making such a major change in one step. While appreciating, however, the advantages of a broader pattern of studies for some pupils (as a step in the right direction) we are apprehensive of the possible consequences of such a measure. There is, in the opinion of those experienced in the realities of university admissions, a risk that the more specialized pattern would be preferred (*de facto*, but not *de jure*) and that the broader pattern of studies would be seen as appropriate mainly to the less academic among sixth-form pupils, and to those whose sixth-form course is not explicitly preparatory for their university course. We would very much regret such a mis-perception of the purpose of broadening the sixth-form curriculum.

I share those concerns.

Moving on from Kenyon's reflections of 1918 to Sir Keith Joseph's priorities today, I am conscious that much of higher educational planning, at least in public sector higher education, is critically conditioned by the following sentence in the Secretary of State's letter to the Chairman of the National Advisory Body's Committee in February 1983:

> When the NAB considers the institutions' plans I hope that, without neglect to the pattern of student demand, priority will be accorded to scientific and technological provision of value to industry, to the operational needs of industry, commerce and the professions, and to meeting the future needs of employers more generally, not least at technician level.

As we approached the completion of NAB's 1984/85 planning exercise, a decision had to be taken about the broad division between subject areas. And although we were conscious of the risk of an abrupt or excessive shift in the system brought about by planners who fail to respect the pattern of informed student demand, we decided to favour the scientific, technological and business studies areas in providing places in our institutions in 1984/85, and to promote a measured shift of the system towards these subjects. I have read – and heard – of concerns that there will be shortages in engineering and computing skills in a few years time because of cutbacks in the university sector. In the local authority sector, we have provided for an extra 15% first-year full-time students in engineering in 1984 compared with 1982, and 47% in maths and computing over the same period. My concern is not whether we have provided sufficient places in these areas, but whether sufficient students will come forward to fill them. And my anxieties increase when I perceive pressure from some departments of government, and from the Engineering Council for a further shift of the system of higher education towards scientific and technological subjects. Nothing will be gained if the universities now expand their provision in these areas and merely attract those candidates for which places have been carefully provided in the polytechnics. The pool of qualifed – and willing – candidates for these subjects is a limited one. We must all note the Secretary of State's balanced advice to NAB, when he asked us not only to give priority to scientific and technological provision, but also not to neglect the pattern of student demand. I have argued elsewhere that the main engine in the planning of higher education should be informed student demand, not manpower planning. And I hold to that view.

What about level, and the length of course? The importance of sub-degree work (the Higher Certificates and Diplomas of the Business and Technician Education Council (BTEC) and the Diploma of Higher Education) has been recognized by NAB from the outset. The balance between such 2-year work and 3-year degrees will remain a critical issue. Are we — following the ideas of the Leverhulme Report — to move to a general introduction of an exclusive initial 2-year qualification? The responses to NAB's consultative exercise on longer-term strategy do not, on the whole, support the idea. Nevertheless, the initial 2-year qualification is not a hypothesis — it is an actual fact for many students today. And public sector higher education (if not the universities, as yet) has to confront the question of striking the right balance between opportunities for the 3-year Honours degree, on the one hand, and for a 2-year course (possibly, but not necessarily, to become a Pass degree) on the other. I believe it will be the special role of some (not a few — but not all) of our institutions in the public sector to concentrate on the provision of 2-year (full-time) initial, advanced further education courses and their longer part-time equivalents, and to link them both backwards to a variety of feeder-routes from non-advanced further education (as well as from secondary education) and forwards by credit-transfer to appropriate degree courses. Our system is sadly short of links and ladders, and we must delay no longer in designing and implementing an effective network of credit-transfer with the aim of ensuring that no one finds himself or herself at the end of an education cul-de sac.

Changes of the kind I have been discussing are essential if we are to develop a policy of extended access to higher education, offering an enhanced provision for part-time students, mature and non-traditional entrants — a policy which assumes that a greater proportion of students will live at home and be served by regional and local institutions. But extended access will not be possible — or possible only to a very limited degree — if we insist on maintaining a high threshold of entry as a characteristic feature of British higher education. We must be prepared to expand provision for the one-A level entrant and welcome those seeking adult and continuing education whose qualifications for admission are in the form of experience rather than certificates. Indeed, I would go further. We need not be too concerned with drop-out rates and failure to complete courses. Where education is working near the margin some drop-out and failure is bound to occur — and it is a mistake to assume that an uncompleted course is a wasted course. Compared to other countries, what are inappropriately termed 'wastage-rates' in Britain are remarkably low. It is to the eternal credit of public sector higher education that it is prepared to work at the margins — to extend the reach of higher education, by providing for the late-developer or the mature student or by exploring and developing new subjects and new methods. It is one of the special tasks of the sector to explore the limits of access and to see how far it is possible to extend opportunities for higher education without sacrificing the quality of the education offered and while maintaining the provision of personal and social and economic benefits. I do not believe we have at all nearly approached these limits yet.

Let me say a further word about quality. The quality of our students is not best measured at the point of entry to higher education. We do not sensibly assess the quality of a rider before he has mounted the horse, or of a pianist before she has learned to play. A levels, and A level grades, are poor predictors of performance in higher education. At the margin, especially, temperament and motivation are more important to success than the prior assimilation of those intellectual skills measured by A level examinations. Quality is inherent in the whole process of higher education − as of education, generally, − and, if it is to be measured, is best assessed at the point of completion.

What is at issue in the debate about the limits of access is not the preservation of institutions or of jobs (sympathetic though one is to those at risk), but rather the provision of the level of qualified manpower the economy will need in the 1990s and beyond, and the development of a more generally educated society. We must make fuller use of the nation's talents. Our concern should be, not that we might be putting at risk the quality of higher education by extending access to it (which I do not believe to be true: more did not mean worse last time, nor will it next time), but rather that we are allowing to go to waste, undeveloped, too much inherent quality in our young people and in our adult population. At the North of England Conference (1984) the Secretary of State spoke of the quest for an improved curriculum and higher standards of attainment in school education. He asked us to consider what our children and young people have it in them to achieve; he reminded us of the challenge of the world into which they are going. What he had to say − which I warmly welcome − is as relevant to the institutions of further and higher education as it is to the schools. And it must not go unheeded.

As we move from the 'seller's market' of the 1980s to what may well be the 'buyer's market' of the 1990s, the question of the limits of useful access to higher education will become critically important. Most of those concerned with admissions to higher education (of which I am one) are more commonly exercised over the question of the suitability (or otherwise) of candidates for particular courses or institutions. We rarely have to face directly the question of whether or not a candidate is suitable for higher education at all. And yet that is the prior question, decided (as often as not) without reference to admissions officers by school-teachers or parents or by the lack of confidence of the marginal candidates themselves.

In addition to the question whether a candidate is suitable for higher education at all, we should also confront the issues involved in the double freedom of admission to higher education institutions in Britain: the freedom of candidates to choose between courses and institutions, and the freedom of teachers (or admissions officers) to choose their own pupils. Should these freedoms be questioned? Has the time come, for example, to consider a national definition of matriculation, to direct more students towards their local institutions (so that they can live at home), or to distribute candidates on a random basis between the institutions offering the chosen course? Such possible limitations on the double freedom of admissions strike one as strange and unattractive, and yet one can readily see advantages in each one of them. Perhaps one should be prepared to contemplate some limited restrictions on them in the future. As a teacher who has for twenty years valued the opportunity to choose my own pupils, I recognize that my freedom to do so has been bought at a high price − not all of which has had to be paid by me.

In recent months I have observed, and played a small part in, two important changes in our systems of admissions in higher education. The Dover Committee's proposals for the reform of the Oxford colleges admissions procedures have now been adopted by all the colleges, and will be implemented for the first time in the autumn of 1985 for admission in 1986. We shall not know until the new system has operated for a year or two how far it will succeed in simplifying admissions from the points of view of the candidate, the school and the tutors. But I am optimistic. Let me welcome also the development of the Polytechnic Central Admissions Scheme, the result of an agreement between the Universities Central Council on Admissions and the Committee of Directors of Polytechnics, with its linked (parallel) system of admissions to full-time and sandwich degree work in universities and the major local authority institutions. This is an imaginative first step towards an integrated system of admissions to United Kingdom higher education. I have no doubt that the scheme should be developed with all deliberate speed to encompass all full-time and sandwich degree work in the different sectors and parts of the United Kingdom. How far it will be appropriate to incorporate degree-equivalent work and sub-degree work is not clear. I doubt whether there will be any advantage to be gained in trying to bring part-time work into such a system. It will be important to remember the needs of the mature student, especially, and to ensure that any general and integrated system of admissions remains fully responsive to the requirements of different kinds of student and of the employer. Above all, it must not be allowed to add a further layer of delay to inhibit the response of higher education to perceived need. One of the most important reasons for seeking a more comprehensive and integrated system of admissions is to provide a better assessment than we have at present of the 'real field' – the pool of qualified and willing candidates for full-time and sandwich courses.

So much for recent developments in higher education and their implications for student admissions. What of the future? Higher education planning has become dominated, if not obsessed, by the issues of resource-constraint and the future demographic decline associated with the low birthrate of the middle 70s. In attempting to plan intelligently for the 1990s, we must first estimate the number and types of student we wish to provide for, then ensure that appropriate courses are designed for them and, finally, plan on an integrated basis the distribution and kinds of institutions we shall need. I have argued that we should plan to satisfy informed student demand rather than attempt (except in special cases) to practise the difficult art of manpower planning. But there is still much to be done to ensure that student demand is properly informed. I have also argued that we urgently need to reconsider the balance between – and the relative prestige of – general courses, more specifically vocational courses, and specialized academic research-related courses. In 1984, as in 1918, there is much to be said for 'proper general education'.

The importance of questions of admissions should not go unrecognized. Like the awards regulations, our systems and procedures of admissions play a major (if often unacknowledged) role in the planning of higher education. And there is one more current, practical and related question that arises. I (for one) welcome the government's intention to introduce I level examinations to provide breadth to A level courses and sixth-form study. Provided that the I level examinations are taken at the same time as the A level, and that the courses are spread over the two years of sixth-form work (and not tidied away and forgotten after one year), they will make an important contribution to securing a general education in our schools. Kenyon, thinking of the candidate for admission to higher education, wanted 'to make it worth his while to keep up his other subjects to some considerable extent up to the end of his school career'. So do I. But only admissions officers — and their masters — have the power to do that. Will they value equally a broader pattern of studies and the more specialized pattern? Or should we ask the Secretary of State to determine centrally a definition of matriculation for higher education which secures once and for all a proper general education in schools?

18
Treasures and Books

In 1984, as summer approached, the National Advisory Body and the University Grants Committee were wrestling with the final stages of determining their strategic advice to the Secretary of State, and negotiating the now famous joint chapter entitled 'Higher Education and the Needs of Society' (Appendix C). What is higher education for? — that seemed to be the fundamental issue. In May I gave the Winton Lecture for 1984 at King Alfred's College, Winchester, and (not entirely fancifully, I hope) linked current issues of educational purpose with King Alfred's great essay on the state of learning in Anglo-Saxon England, offering several different answers to the wider question: what is education for?

There is a story — apocryphal, no doubt — that when Sir Keith Joseph took up his appointment as Secretary of State for Education and Science in 1981, he insisted on asking various members of his new department the question: What is education *for?* — and they found it difficult to provide a satisfactory answer. My readers may smile — but on the condition that they have an adequate answer ready. Educational theorists (and educational economists) — setting aside for the moment the advancement of learning and research — tell us that the functions of education are threefold: *skills, socialization* and *sorting*. It is customary nowadays to divide the concept of educational skills into specific disciplinary or vocational skills, on the one hand, and general (or 'transferable') skills, on the other. We know (more or less) — or think we know — what is meant by the disciplinary skills of (say) chemistry or computer science or Chinese — while acknowledging uneasily that it would be more difficult to specify the disciplinary skills of English, or economics or engineering. And the idea of vocational skills — whether of teaching, or medicine, or librarianship, or catering, or graphic design — is not hard to grasp. Transferable skills, or 'the general powers of the mind', however, are something which it is a good deal easier to assert than to analyse — let alone to examine rigorously. Employers — who (rightly) set a high value on transferable skills — often describe them in terms of communication, problem-solving and teamwork. Most courses in British higher education offer opportunities (often indirectly, rather than directly) for the development of communication skills and problem-solving skills: but opportunities for the development of the inter-personal skills (implied in the phrase 'teamwork') are less commonly found as part of a course. It is often the social and cultural life of students (including political activity and sport) that provides them with an informal education in inter-personal skills and teamwork.

What I want to stress is the gulf that is set at present between academics (on the one hand) who classify — and think about — education primarily in terms of disciplinary and vocational skills and the employers (on the other) for whom transferable skills and attitude are as important — if not, more important. My colleague David Bradshaw (Principal of the Doncaster Metropolitan Institute of Higher Education) has suggested to me that we should examine more precisely what we mean when we claim — as I do — that all courses of higher education develop general powers of the mind. How are we to analyse, and classify, transferable skills? Borrowing from American work, we might start by listing five essential elements: (1) the skills of communication (verbal and non-verbal); (2) quantitative competence (knowing how to use, and when not to use, quantitative techniques); (3) analytic skills — to which Sir Keith Joseph referred in 1984 when he argued that the study of history is valuable not least because it teaches people 'to use their reason as well as their memories, and to develop skills of analysis and criticism in a situation where there cannot be a provably right answer'; (4) synthesizing skills — the ability to integrate and unify diffuse bodies of information (this rare and valuable skill, well described in C.P. Snow's novel, *The Search*, is not sufficiently encouraged or developed in our educational system, which sets so high a value on analytic skills and specialized study); (5) the clarification of values — how do we determine (in St Paul's words) 'whatsoever things are true, whatsoever things are honest, whatsoever things are just, whatsoever things are pure, whatsoever things are lovely, whatsoever things are of good report' ...?

If we could develop an acceptable system for the categorization of transferable skills, it might then be possible to see which disciplines (and which courses) develop which skills. We might also be able to see where there are deficiencies and think about correcting them. Could it be that historians and English students are deficient in quantitative skills? Are chemists and computer scientists often enough confronted with questions of value?

But what is all this irrelevant talk about 'transferable skills'? What has it got to do with treasures and books? I am — of course — trying to offer an answer to the Secretary of State's question ('What is education for?'), and to discover some fundamental principles, though I realize that what I call fundamental principles others may recognize as basic prejudices.

Skills, socialization and sorting: the three functions of education. What is meant by socialization? Human beings — with a few exceptions — are not solitary creatures: they live and work in societies — families, schools, colleges, clubs and communes, tribes and teams, firms, unions, parties, quangos, churches and nations. And we have to learn to develop a complex and appropriate social competence to become an effective member of these groups. Think about the demands made upon us by a Sunday meal at home, or a seminar at college, an assembly line — or a strike, a committee or a cricket match, self-government or war. Not only the world of employment, but society itself (if it aspires to be effective and content), looks to education to develop qualities and attitudes such as tolerance, co-operation, disin-terestedness and self reliance. 'Here is a task for all that a man has of fortitude and delicacy' — Stevenson's comment is about family life, but it will do as well for any social group. For our predecessors, this socializing function of education gave a serious and well-argued basis for such things as boarding schools and team-games, residential colleges, formal dinners and compulsory chapel — where we are called upon to pray that men and women 'may honour one another, and seek the common good'. Some of these expressions of educational theory are out of fashion today: and where that is so, it may be that we should find new and appropriate forms through which to realize the socializing function of education. For the function remains: the need for socialization is no less in the twentieth century than it was in the nineteenth.

Critics of this idea refer to it as the 'baby-sitting' theory of education, implying that it defines the function of education in terms of containment, pacification — the crushing of the distinctive and (often) delightful variety of our children and our students into a dull and sullen conformity. Not so. It is, of course, the case that in contemporary Britain employment prospects for young people are bleak — especially during those difficult years between the ages of 16 and 21. And it is one of the tasks of our educational system to provide a valid and rewarding alternative to — and preparation for — the world of employment. While not for one moment forgetting the equal needs of adult and continuing education, this represents a major challenge to those of us who work in further and higher education, in central and local government, in the National Advisory Body and the Manpower Services Commission. Some 1100 years ago in the city of Winchester King Alfred, in a document which may be described as the first royal commission on education in England, suggested simply that the youth of the nation, 'should be set to study, for as long as they are of no other use'. Alfred's idea of education clearly marries the achievement of skills (literacy in the vernacu-lar, and in Latin) with socialization.

But in our diverse, multi-cultural, changing society — with formal and informal dissent as one of its most remarkable features — the socializing function of education is a difficult and delicate question. It is certainly not to be defined as the teaching of conformity. Rather — in a nation proud of its history of bloodless revolutions — its aim should be to form citizens of a society which can tolerate dissent and accommodate change without either violence or breakdown.

The third function of education I wish to consider is the sorting function. Society — and the employers — look to education to sort and classify young people (and adults) into convenient categories — for example, those who leave school or college without formal qualifications, those with CSEs, those with GCEs at O level or A level, those with degrees (themselves further sub-classified) and those with postgraduate qualifications. Let me say at once that I believe this to be one of the least efficient and least satisfactory aspects of our educational system — first, because there is altogether too much sorting, classifying and examination built into the system; secondly, because our sorting processes try to do too much (and perhaps fail to do anything well) — they are expected to establish the rigour of the antecedent course, to select for the succeeding stage of education, and to offer a preliminary sorting of the labour force for the employers; thirdly, because our examinations are such poor predictors of performance in later stages of education – let alone in later life and in employment. A level grades are not good predictors of degree classes; degree classes are not good predictors of career achievement. In this respect, I welcome the Secretary of State's decision to introduce Advanced Supplementary (AS) level examinations alongside A levels in the belief that they will help to produce broader general education in sixth forms, and a more sensitive and useful sorting for the world of employment – as well as for higher education.

Beside the overt and formal systems of assessment in education, there exists a covert and informal and (wholly pernicious) system based on institutions. Pupils and students from one school, or college, or university are preferred to those from another – merely because of the reputation of the institutions, and regardless of the achievement or potential of the individual. There is now plenty of evidence that this kind of informal sorting is inefficient and harmful to our society. Even where it seems to operate reasonably satisfactorily (except for those rejected) – as in some traditional professions – it appears to provide no more than (at best) a self-fulfilling prophecy.

All these points of weakness are to be found in the sorting function of British education at present – and they need attention, but one of the most serious weaknesses of contemporary educational sorting has still to be mentioned: this is its academic bias. In brief, our sorting systems of highest prestige are biased toward disciplinary skills and away from vocational skills; they take insufficient account of general or transferable skills; and they favour academic and critical studies to the disadvantage of practical or creative abilities. Can we doubt this? Do we value equally an A level in mathematics and in woodwork? an Honours degree in philosophy, in design, or in dance? We must learn to recognize more clearly the value (to the individual and to society) of the City and Guilds qualifications, for example, and the work of the Business and Technician Education Council (BTEC), and to treat them with the same respect accorded to A levels and degrees.

What is education for? I have tried to explore an answer to that question in terms of three functions: skills, socialization, and sorting. In each case the analysis has suggested inadequacies: in particular, the domination of our educational thinking by disciplinary and vocational skills to the detriment and neglect of general or transferable skills; the failure to address in modern terms the issue of the socializing function of education; and the pronounced academic bias of the sorting function. Let no one think that in saying this I am questioning the need for the pursuit of excellence, or the maintenance and enhancement of quality, but the critical question is this: quality in respect of what?

We must start by determining what higher education is for. It is appropriate in this connection to look back to Lord Robbins's great report of 1963 and to recall its four objectives for a properly balanced system of higher education:

i　*instruction in skills* suitable to play a part in the general division of labour;

ii　*but* what is taught should be taught in such a way as to promote *the general powers of the mind*;

iii *the advancement of learning*;
iv *the transmission of a common culture and common standards of citizenship.*

But I want to go back far beyond the Royal Commission which reported over the signature of Lord Robbins in 1963 to that first royal report on national education, which is to be found in King Alfred's preface to his translation of Gregory's *Pastoral Care.* I have already referred to his proposal for elementary education in the reading and writing of English, with selective — more advanced — education in Latin. I am afraid that even the elementary system was to be discriminatory by class (and, no doubt, by sex) and not grant-aided: only the children of free men with sufficient resources were to be educated. Still, it was a start...and we must yet play our part to carry it forward. What were they to study? Alfred tells us that he and his learned colleagues set to work to translate into English (as basic text-books) 'some books which are most needful for all men to know'. A core curriculum! What would we have chosen to translate for this purpose in 891 in the midst of a bitter war with the Danish invaders? What would we choose today? Apart from the Bible, Alfred selected Gregory's *Pastoral Care, The Consolation of Philosophy* by Boethius, and two books of history — one of the world and one of the English nation. I doubt whether he lived to complete his scheme — and we do not know the whole of it — but here in outline are the four categories of Lord Robbins: instruction in skills (literacy), concern for the general powers of the mind, the advancement of learning, and (above all) the transmission of a common culture and common standards of citizenship. Perhaps we should conclude that these things are needful for all men (and all women) in every generation.

King Alfred remembered happier times than his own, before the Danish invasions, when the great monastic houses 'stood filled with treasures and books'. They had been neglected, and then destroyed. He started again, circulating copies of his books to each of his bishops and attaching a treasured object to each copy. The book that was sent to Worcester survives to this day in the Bodleian Library at Oxford: one of those treasures (the Alfred Jewel found in Athelney Marshes) can be seen in the Ashmolean Museum in the same city...*Treasures and Books*. What are the particular treasures and the special books in our schools and colleges and polytechnics and universities today? What is our education for? I have offered several answers to that question: let me try once more.

To be fully happy — to be fully human — beyond mere existence, we need three things which only education can give: *role, aspiration* and *ideal*. Everyone needs a role in society in which he or she can feel comfortable and achieve self-respect. (It is not necessarily true that such a role is equivalent for all members of society to full-time paid employment in adult life, though our society has come very close to adopting this heresy.) Everyone needs an aspiration — to be, to achieve, to win, to create, to discover something as yet out of reach, but not unreachable. Everyone needs an ideal (or an idol), an object of devotion, someone or something other, some cause or some idea, which can be served or loved or worshipped. I should wish to define the function of education in these terms: to help us to determine, and to find, our roles — our aspirations — our ideals. This is what education is for. Or so I think. It is, of course, a question everyone must answer for himself or herself. If we are not satisfied with the three categories of *skills, socialization* and *sorting*, or with the Robbins definition of the objectives of higher education, or King Alfred's idea of treasures and books (most needful for all men to know), or my own account in terms of *role, aspiration* and *ideal*, we must provide another answer, and one which we can defend and realize. For unless the Secretary of State's question is answered, it is hard to see how teachers and lecturers can function effectively. And the same goes for those of us engaged in educational planning, such as the members of NAB or the UGC.

When we know what higher education is for, we will know more clearly how many places to provide for the students of the future. The number of full-time and part-time students expected to seek higher education in the years to come is, of course, the point of departure for future planning. Many people seem to believe that this is a question of statistics. And so it is — in part. But demand for higher education — and access to it — are managed, not natural, processes. And all statistical projections rest upon policy assumptions — which can be questioned. Nevertheless, reflecting on the 'damping effect' of part-time numbers — which tend to grow as full-time students become scarce (and vice versa) — and upon other factors, I believe that overall student demand is likely to remain more or less constant (for longer than we have been led to expect by some forecasts) perhaps right through to the end of the decade. And the descent, when it comes, will be shallower and less severe than we have feared.

However, is it really satisfactory to make estimates for future demand for advanced further education (AFE) without also taking into account non-advanced further education (NAFE)? It is a commonplace — and one of the principles upon which NAB's planning is founded — that AFE and NAFE form a seamless web and in many institutions support one another's existence and benefit from one another's presence. One looks forward to the time when the local education authorities, the DES and the MSC can come together to achieve forward planning in NAFE in co-operation with NAB which has this responsibility for AFE. At such a time we might be able to explore a comprehensive policy for the further and higher education of young people over 16, and for adult and continuing education. What would such a policy consist in? In view of what I have said about the functions of education, I hope we might contemplate the establishment of a 'citizen's right' to further (or advanced further) education — not necessarily or always fully grant-aided — and extend the Robbins principle to allow *all those who wanted it* to have the means of access to NAFE or AFE, as appropriate.

If we are to look for wider access to further education (including AFE) then NAB must develop a working relationship with those responsible for NAFE (including the employers) at least as effective as the one already forged with the UGC. For the students we wish to attract — and to provide for — both now and in the future will not all by any means require (or be suited to) courses modelled on the university pattern. The specialized, research-related, full-time Honours degree is a fine thing, but it should not be our only model of excellence. As long ago as 1906 Reginald Lane Poole was reflecting on the strength of what he called 'the Oxford system': he perceived 'the immense power of accumulated tradition'. The attractive force of the university model — reinforced often by the requirements of the professional bodies – creates academic drift in public sector higher education. We need an alternative model of excellence to act as a counterweight: perhaps the Open University, or the idea of community colleges, can be developed to fulfil this role. In any event, if we are to make adequate provision for sub-degree work in AFE, for the needs of part-time students, for adult and continuing education, and for those students whose work is near the (arbitrary and unreal) boundary between AFE and NAFE, those of us responsible for public sector higher education must help to promote and to develop (besides the full-time degree) courses which will exemplify alternative models of excellence, of equal prestige. We cannot afford to be half-hearted about this – for where your heart is, there is your treasure also.

More than half of the full-time equivalent students in higher education in England are now being educated outside the universities – in polytechnics, colleges and institutes of higher education. There is nothing wrong with a national system of higher education in which the majority of the students are in public sector institutions – provided that the education offered is appropriate, the resources adequate, the status not inferior and the quality satisfactory. As NAB proceeds in the future to plan the majority sector of higher education, it will need to pay particular attention to the question of the provision of *appropriate education, adequate resources, equal status* and *high quality*. These are issues both for the planning body and for the institutions.

Faced with the resource-constraints of the 80s, and the demographic trends at 18+ in the 90s, institutions – like the planning bodies – must address the issue of fitness for purpose. I doubt whether the idea of excellence in education has much meaning unless it is related to educational purpose. We must all answer the Secretary of State's question: What is education for?

19

What the Hell is Quality?

'Quality in education' is a subject extraordinarily difficult to come to grips with, and full of pitfalls. There is no single final answer to the quality question, and we should not look for it. But the issue cannot be avoided. My provisional conclusion, put forward here in a paper read at a conference at Manchester Polytechnic in October 1984, is that the best way to address it is to ask 'Quality for what?' Quality is fitness for purpose.

Quality: we know what it is, yet we don't know what it is. But that is self-contradictory, for some things are better than others: that is, they have more quality. But when you try to say what the quality is, apart from the things that have it, it all goes 'poof'. There's nothing to talk about. But if you can't say what quality is, how do you know what it is, or how do you know that it even exists? If no-one knows what it is, then for all practical purposes, it doesn't exist at all. But for all practical purposes, it really does exist. What else are the grades based on? Why else would people pay fortunes for some things and throw others in the trash pile? Obviously some things are better than others. But what's the betterness? So round and round you go, spinning mental wheels, and nowhere finding any place to get traction. What the hell is quality? what is it?

Let me offer two more quotations to add to Pirsig's from *Zen and the Art of Motorcycle Maintenance*. First the National Advisory Body to the Secretary of State (9 November 1983):

The Committee has stressed its desire to have available to it the best possible advice on quality: not only on particular programmes of work, but also whole institutions,

and ten days later, on 19 December 1983, the Secretary of State in reply:

I welcome the progressive strengthening of the capacity to bring quality judgements to bear in the planning process.

I suspect that quality in higher education will prove to be the major issue of my second term of office with NAB, just as resources have obviously been the major issue of the first three years.

Let me stress that the topic is complicated by three of its basic aspects. First, it is undoubtedly very difficult. Intellectually and academically this is one of the most difficult ventures we might undertake — to try and define what we mean by quality in higher education and what we can do about it. One has to beware of those who think they have easy answers, for they are almost certainly wrong (or 'incomplete' would perhaps be a better description).

Second, I am in no doubt of the sensitivity of engaging in a debate on the question of quality in higher education (particularly when NAB enters on the subject). Political in every sense of the word; it is a subject that the Secretary of State cares about deeply, though he, like the rest of us, finds it difficult to articulate exactly what he means. It is also, of course, enormously sensitive within an institution, among members of staff, among students — and, when a planning body starts talking about quality in higher education, everyone fears the worst.

Third, quality is important. It cannot in my view be left aside: it has to be tackled. It has to be tackled by NAB, but NAB cannot take it on alone. We need advice on quality.

Why should we bother with the question of quality at all in NAB? Would it be possible for a national planning body to say 'Yes of course there is an issue of quality in higher education, but it is not for us; we don't need to bother with it, someone else can think about what they mean by the quality of the students; the planning body can do without it.' I do not think that anybody has actually firmly articulated that kind of advice to NAB. In any event, the quotations from NAB's Committee and the Secretary of State make it clear that it would not be possible for NAB to manage without addressing the issue of quality in higher education. A body that plans the pattern of institutions and of courses on grounds merely (and I emphasize 'merely') of regional distribution, of demand from students, of needs of employers, and of cheapness would simply not do a good job. Surely there is one other criterion missing from that check list: that is, the quality of the work. And indeed, again and again, NAB is told that it cannot do its job without assuring itself that it has properly assessed the comparative quality of the candidates and has chosen to build on strength. At NAB's very first Board Residential meeting in October 1982, when we were still being set up, three main topics were discussed: the need for a regional policy, the need for a research policy, and the need to address the issue of quality. We now have a regional policy, and we have delivered the research policy.

Quality. That is our Achilles' Heel. We have been talking about quality ever since 1982 and bringing it to bear again and again on decision-making; but we have always run into difficulties. It is a sensitive issue, and nothing will take away that sensitivity. For example, look at the Town Planning exercise of 1983. The Secretariat drew up proposals for town planning courses which used a range of criteria and gave considerable weight both to regional distribution and to the importance of maintaining part-time provision: the proposals took some account of quality. Like a lot of NAB's work, it was a piece of advice based on a mix of criteria. The Board threw the proposals out, asking that the exercise be done again, primarily on the basis of quality; saying that it was important to find the best courses and preserve them, and correspondingly find the weaker courses and close them. We did just that. The result was a considerable outcry and upheaval in the system, which is what will no doubt happen again next time.

In January 1984 a paper on quality was written for NAB's Board, and we again tried to define what we meant by it, and how we could deal with it more carefully. It was debated whether NAB should undertake its own formal visits to institutions in order to address the question directly; the matter is still lying on the table, as yet undecided. There are very good reasons for saying that no NAB programme of visits should be undertaken, and one of the most significant is the cry of 'Oh no, not more visits!' I can well understand that, but institutions must realize that there is a contradiction in asking NAB to take account of quality whilst denying it the opportunity of making intelligent quality assessments for itself.

Meanwhile, the research policy coming forward from NAB's Committee is highly selective and is based on a careful consideration of the quality (in respect of both past performance and future potential) of research work in institutions and, indeed, in departments within institutions. It is a good example of a NAB policy which critically depends on addressing the issue of quality. We have also considered a limited intervention in the area of biotechnology, a highly selective exercise which threw up three positive proposals for development, again dependent upon quality. The latter was a very different approach of course from that regarding research – it was at a more specific level – but, as before, relative judgements had to be made.

My first question,'Why bother with quality in NAB?' is, I hope, easily answered. We have to, and we want to, and we should take account of quality. It did not take NAB long from the very outset to recognize the truth of that assertion.

The second question to be asked is 'Who can advise NAB?' Where should we look for advice? First, we look to HM Inspectorate: HMI are in membership of NAB, not assessors, and they have a responsibility to advise us (as they advise the Secretary of State) regarding the quality of work done in our institutions. Second, we look towards the validators. Here of course there is a whole debate on the subject of NAB's relations with the validators and NAB's request for quality advice, which must mean *relative* quality advice, if it is to be helpful. Questions have been raised both within the institutions and by the validators themselves, as to the appropriateness of asking advice in this quarter, since the validators are operating *threshold* not relative quality assessment. I take the view that their membership of NAB is not for decorative purposes, and that they are, after HMI, the experts on quality in the public sector. If they were not asked for quality advice, relative or threshold, they would give it anyway, and rightly so: they cannot have been validating for all these years without developing something of an expertise. It would be an extraordinary world where BTEC, CNAA and – to a lesser extent – the university validators were actually prevented or discouraged from having their say on all the delicate issues of quality that arise.

Third, we look to the accreditors and the professional bodies, and this is where there has been a weakness in NAB's operation so far. We can name the professional bodies and we can develop relations with them, but the accreditors have played quite a small part in the quality assessment of courses so far. Perhaps the best example has been in architecture, where the professional body concerned has taken a leading part in bringing NAB's recent report forward: but closer and more structured relations are still sought with the accreditors.

The fourth source of advice on quality is in the institutions themselves. It goes without saying that any institution must be given the opportunity to make a case about its own quality. However, it also goes almost without saying that one can only rest so much weight on somebody speaking for their own case.

The fifth source of advice on quality is in NAB's own procedures. Here the possibility of NAB visitations arises again. Should we start a cycle of structured visits to institutions? Should we try to get round every three years in order to fit in with planning exercises? Every five years in order to fit in with what is humanly possible? Every seven years (which would not impress anyone)? And should we visit *all* the institutions or just the major ones? One is then thrown into the problem of defining a major institution, and pressed up against some more of the unresolved questions that still lie on the agenda.

The third question on quality itself is 'Quality in respect of what?' If we are going to talk about quality we must start by breaking the word down into its component parts. What in fact are we talking of? Since NAB advises the Secretary of State on his powers of course approval, we must know something about the quality of courses from time to time. We need to know about the quality of departments, particularly if we are developing a research policy and seeking to develop the idea of focusing work in some areas. Quality of programmes of work is yet a little wider: where, for instance, have certain programmes done well and where have they done less well? NAB needs to feel its way towards having a sense of the quality of whole programmes, where one can talk about coherent programmes.

Quality in respect of institutions is probably the most difficult judgement to make, both for the present and the future. The future presents particular problems not just concerning the continual resource constraints which we must expect from the present government (and indeed from any likely successor) but also because of the downward demographic trends of the 1990s (on whatever assessment is made). When that occurs the question of institutional quality will surely come to the fore since there is a fair chance that the higher education system will need to be rationalized.

Quality in respect of what? In respect of resources? We certainly need to know about the quality of an institution's physical resources – the libraries, laboratories, buildings. Quality in respect of staff? Perhaps this is the most painful issue to address, but a planning body has to ask itself where the staff are good, and where they are less good. And if we did not do that whilst we were at the same time trying to invest for the future on the basis of strength, staff would be the first to complain. And quality of students? We need an assessment of the quality of students. So the word quality, when unpacked, reveals the number of different questions that arise regarding quality in courses, departments, programmes, institutions, resources, staff, and students. All these need to be addressed.

The analysis of quality is in no sense a single valued exercise. There is no single dimension of quality of the sort that I think the general public would like to have, on which you would be able to locate institution X at the top, Y in the middle, and Z at the bottom and say that you had sorted out quality in higher education. That is not the picture at all. Quality subsumes a number of interlocking, cross-cutting criteria, which make the picture extraordinarily complex. It is in taking account of this difficult construct and marrying it in with other criteria (cost, regional distribution, student demand, and national need), that a planning body finds the issue of quality a very slippery thing to get hold of.

In developing an analysis of quality, we must make the distinction between value and excellence. Wrapped up in the word quality are two quite different, but nevertheless interlocking, measurements which can be teased out of it by looking at a word implicit in it, 'good'. The word good has at least two important senses. When we talk about a good sword, we are not making a moral judgement about the sword: we just mean that the sword is 'rather good at the job': it kills people when we want to kill people. It is a competent, effective sword but not a morally good sword: we are not saying it is valuable in a moral sense. When we talk about a good man, however, we usually mean the other kind of good. We are not referring to him as being competent or effective, but we are talking about his moral qualities. We talk of the value of a good man, and the excellence of a good sword.

Value and excellence both lie in quality and they are both important, but they are two very different issues. In the climate in which we live we could say that the student who had been through an engineering course and achieved third class Honours was valuable to British industry, but that he had not achieved excellence on the course. Conversely, we might say that the student who followed a course in my own subject, English, and achieved first class Honours was excellent at his course, but that he was less valuable to the society in which we now live than was the other student. Of course, my example is open to debate, but it is the distinction that I want to insist on not the example. We must be clear whether we are talking about excellence or value, or both; and we need to know about both before we make planning decisions.

For the planner quality is never a thing of the past. In higher education the measurable things are often already a year (and sometimes two years) out of date by the time they get to a national planning body. Some people believe that it is important to count PhDs on the academic staff and compute that as a proportion, or, using the UCCA system, to count the A level scores of the students at intake, items that are quite easily measurable, although the information is not available for at least a year after the event. But the planning body is planning for a period two, perhaps as much as ten, years in the future, so that the quality assessment it is looking for is not concerned with what the institution and the course, staff and students looked like two years ago, but what they are going to be like in two or more years time. We must be careful of making judgements on assessments of past quality, and assuming that they will apply in the future.

In this list of cautions must be included a warning not to overvalue the measurable indices. Most of these are tempting, but they are will-o-the-wisps. Counting the PhDs of staff in order to assure oneself of staff quality is known by those who teach in higher education or manage higher education to be a crude, simplistic and misleading criterion, for it does not address the question 'Staff effectiveness for what?'. Equally, measuring the A level quality of students by using the UCCA system which is so beloved in universities (and upon which we understand that the University Grants Committee has rested some of its planning) just will not do. It is not informative, and in a sector which makes a virtue, as it should, of seeking out students who have lost educational opportunities at earlier periods and students of promise rather than of performance, students who are mature but have no A levels (or who have not got many of them or have not got them with good grades), to start counting UCCA scores at A level and make planning decisions on that basis would be very foolish indeed.

NAB will not do this, and we will not be particularly impressed by institutions which collect such evidence and tell us that that is a measure of their own excellence. We must be a little subtler than that, perhaps by encouraging institutions to think in terms of value added. 'Value added' takes as given the students as they were on entry and concerns itself with the question of how good they were when they went out. Can one, then, measure value added? If so, the institution that takes in a student with two Es at A level and turns out somebody with a second class Honours degree is scoring very high on value added, whereas the students at my own college in Oxford who come in with extraordinarily high A level grades but sometimes go out, alas, with low seconds or even thirds, would suggest that the college is not doing very well in terms of value added.

We must not be afraid of making judgements. Judgements constitute one of the reasons why quality is so sensitive and embarrassing, but at the end of the day you have to make human judgements about it. And in doing so, I would caution against using too few criteria. We are more likely to get our quality judgements right if we keep approaching them from different points of view than if we base them on some single measure (which will certainly prove something but perhaps not what we were really after).

Above all, when selecting criteria, we must select the appropriate ones for the purpose. Quality judgements do not take place in a vacuum: the question is Quality for what? To find the right institutions to put special research funds into? To determine which are the best art and design courses on which to build for the future (recognizing that that can only be done by terminating some others, because there are not the funds available to keep everything going)? We must look for appropriate criteria.

Finally, we must not confuse the *necessary* conditions for quality with *sufficient* conditions. We in NAB have had a very interesting debate on the question of 'critical mass'.The question before us was 'Is there a minimum level for an institution, a department, or a group of staff which can properly support work of reasonable quality in higher education, and which would then create a planning base from which we could work?' The evidence we have is that there is a proper approach to planning which recognizes that, at the departmental level (and that begs all the questions that arise on how one defines a department) there is probably a minimum effective size of group for high quality work. If institutions let departments fall below that level (though the number may be different for different departments) work will probably fall in quality. It is therefore a necessary condition for good quality work that departments are of a buoyant size. Some departments can be quite small — five or six members — and still be buoyant, whilst for other subjects, the evidence we have before us seems to suggest that departmental sizes have to be rather bigger, that the critical mass has to be bigger for the necessary conditions of quality to develop.

If that view prevails and is found to be sound, much more work needs to be done on it to make it into an effective planning tool. It will, of course, have a bearing on the question of the 'critical mass' of an institution. A small institution might well be viable if its range of work is restricted; a large institution, on the other hand, might well be non-viable if its range of work is in fact such as to produce a large number of departments below the effective critical mass. We can approach the ideas of effective departmental size and the necessary conditions for quality work, and then focus on the work of institutions and thereby arrive at the idea of viable sizes for institutions. Here is a potentially coherent body of thought, but one which needs to be more fully worked out.

What I have been discussing are the necessary but not the sufficient conditions for quality. Certainly in institutions, once one has created the necessary conditions, the question then arises how can one go on and create the sufficient conditions for real quality work? The critical remaining question relates to *fitness for purpose*. Ask institutions whether they can show fitness for purpose. Ask course leaders whether they can show fitness for purpose in the course, then we will be confronting the real issue of quality.

20

Public Sector Universities

Graduation speeches are never easy to judge. One tries (I suppose) to congratulate the graduates and diplomates without embarrassing them, to inform their families and friends without boring them, and to encourage the academic staff without misleading them. On the occasion of the Hatfield Polytechnic graduation ceremony in November 1984 I particularly wanted to address the issue of the titles we give to public sector institutions: colleges and polytechnics or (perhaps) universities? I have come to feel that public sector higher education, now the majority sector in England, is not sufficiently visible — to the public, potential students, their families, employers, and indeed the press and television — and so not sufficiently valued. How can this be remedied if not by giving the major institutions the title university?

The National Advisory Body's success is not its own: it is the success of public sector higher education, an important part of which is the system of thirty polytechnics in England and Wales. It is a success born of a steadfast devotion to educational purpose. Let me remind you what public sector higher education is for. 'The major contribution of the public sector is to the teaching and community purposes of higher education with the emphasis on providing access to all who might benefit.' I do not believe we have nearly reached the limit of providing access for all who might benefit, and I dream of a day when the question is not whether 14 or 15% (or 20 or 25%) of the 18+ age group should receive higher education, but when we achieve a truly comprehensive system of further and higher education for adults and school-leavers alike. 'Trust in your dreams, not in statistics', said William Saroyan.

For education, in particular higher education, properly understood is a pearl of great price. Thomas Traherne, the seventeenth-century poet and mystic, who was educated in my own university at Oxford, wrote about the impact and delight of higher education (and I am grateful to Professor John Dancy for drawing my attention to this):

Having been at the University and received there the taste and tincture of another education, I saw that there were things in this world of which I never dreamed, glorious secrets and glorious persons past imagination. There I saw that logic, ethics, physics, metaphysics, geometry, astronomy, poesy, medicine, grammar, music, rhetoric, all kinds of arts, trades and mechanicisms that adorned the world pertained to felicity. At least there I saw those things, which afterwards I knew to pertain unto it: and was delighted in it. There I saw into the nature of the sea, the heavens, the sun, the moon and stars, the elements, minerals, vegetables all which appeared like the King's daughter, all glorious within, and those things which my nurses and parents should have talked of, there were taught unto me.

But wonder and delight, the foundations of wisdom, are not in themselves enough. There is still the greatest question to address and answer — the one my children put succinctly in the words: So what? Purpose — What is it all for? — So what? I am one of those who believe that 'all meaningful thought is for the sake of action'.

Traherne's account of 'the taste and tincture of another education' which he found at Oxford is followed by some words which are critical of the university. He goes on:

Nevertheless some things were defective too. We studied to inform our knowledge but knew not to what end we studied. And for lack of arriving at a certain end, we erred in the manner.

Whether we are students or teachers or governors or planners, we would do well to ponder the question that Traherne raises. What are your educational purposes? What are mine?

Karl Marx wrote 'the point is not to understand the world but to change it.' I find those impatient words of his challenging and stimulating, but would rather say that the point of advanced study — in a college, or polytechnic or university — is to understand the world precisely so that we may change it. Such is the vision which the best students have before them.

As I contemplate our world and our nation today I am insistently reminded of W.H. Auden's poem *September 1, 1939*:

> I and the public know
> What all schoolchildren learn,
> Those to whom evil is done
> Do evil in return ...
>
> For the error bred in the bone
> Of each woman and each man
> Craves what it cannot have,
> Not universal love
> But to be loved alone ...
>
> There is no such thing as the State
> And no-one exists alone;
> Hunger allows no choice
> To the citizen or the police;
> We must love one another or die.

We must love one another or die. If we have not yet understood this, we have missed the most important lesson of our lives. So we must not lose heart (though some who should know better are doing so) — we should not lose heart in higher education if the gross national product shows a temporary fall, or if the truly equal society seems still a distant dream, or if graduates and lecturers seem no better than other men and women: those things, though desirable, were never what higher education was for. What is it for? To understand the world precisely so that we may change it.

A system of higher education which is, and seeks to be, both purposeful and diverse must be dynamic. Far from being afraid of change, it should welcome it, and constantly respond to the challenge of a developing world and a changing society. At Keble we have on the external wall of the college perhaps Oxford's most famous piece of graffiti: a long sleepy-looking dinosaur skilfully executed in white paint over red brick. The college staff, although instructed to clean off all other graffiti, are not allowed to remove the college dinosaur — and indeed undergraduates (with connivance of the Warden) creep out at night and touch up the outline with fresh paint when it becomes worn or dim. Underneath this noble beast is inscribed the following: *Remember what happened to the dinosaur.* Not a bad motto for an Oxford College! Not a bad piece of advice for a polytechnic or a university. Not a bad warning to British higher education in general. And here, in terms of responsiveness to the need to change, public sector higher education has a good record and sets an impressive example to the university sector. But further change is, no doubt, necessary, and will be required of us not only by external constraints — of demographic changes, patterns of employment (or unemployment), and limited resources — but also by a redefined and rediscovered sense of purpose and objective in higher education.

There are some who believe that when we come to face the challenges ahead of us, the university sector will be preferred to the public sector. I do not. There are some who predict that the distinctive education offered (at their best) by the polytechnics and the local authority and voluntary colleges will be swept aside by crude power-politics in the DES. I do not. No higher education institution need fear for its future, which is devoted to educational purpose and purposeful education, which is responsive to changing national, regional and local needs, which is of unquestioned high quality, and which is provenly cost-effective. That is a high aim, but whether we serve in the universities or the public sector, we owe our students nothing less. For our students are, of course, the raison d'être of higher education.

And let me say unequivocally that I believe that our students in public sector higher education have earned — and deserve — parity of status with their fellow-students in the universities. Some of my colleagues on the Board of NAB have concluded that parity of status cannot be achieved without a change of institutional title — that there cannot be a fair competition for able candidates, that employers will never offer equal opportunities to our graduates, that the general public will not learn to value properly the public sector, unless our polytechnics (and some few major colleges) are retitled universities — public sector universities. I am impressed by their arguments and believe that they have raised a timely issue which NAB will in due course need to address. I should hope that the government would be prepared to give the most serious conideration to a well-argued case. But, if the retitling of our major public sector institutions is seen as an excuse for slipping the reins of validation and the discipline of quality assurance — then I oppose it. If it is intended as a device to allow academic drift away from part-time and sub-degree work, and from responsiveness to the local and regional needs of employers — than I oppose it. If it is understood as a step towards removing our major institutions from local authority control — then I oppose it. The first responsibility of public sector institutions is to provide access for the local and regional community. I repeat: 'The major contribution of the public sector is to the teaching and community purposes of higher education with the emphasis on providing access to all who might benefit.'

We must not forget two significant points: first, that public sector higher education is now the majority sector of English higher education. It is neither natural nor appropriate to deny to the institutions containing the majority of our students the normal title of institutions of higher education in Britain. And, secondly, on the North American continent the term university is used more generously, less grudgingly — and with no obvious harm. The issue, in the end, is a simple one of justice for our students. When — and if — I come to believe that the most effective way to achieve parity of status and esteem for our students is to retitle our public sector institutions, I shall unhesitatingly join those who are calling for the title *university*.

Postscript

On the last day of December 1984 I completed five years as head of Keble College, and one month later my first three years as Chairman of the Board of the National Advisory Body came to an end. What next? For Keble – a pioneering college – (as ever) the way ahead is in the redefinition and recreation in modern terms of the essentials of an Oxford collegiate education – admission on merit to an international community, tutorial teaching, scholarship (without its tyranny!) and the ultimate purpose of service to the nation in the world of employment (see Appendix D). For NAB and public sector higher education the challenge is no less, and not so different – to explore the limits of access without compromising the standards of British higher education, to create a lasting triple alliance with government and the world of employent, to achieve truly integrated planning across the increasingly unreal and hampering boundaries of nation, sector and educational phase. Can it be done? 'Trust in your dreams, not in statistics. ...'

Appendix A

The National Advisory Body

TERMS OF REFERENCE OF THE COMMITTEE FOR LOCAL AUTHORITY HIGHER EDUCATION JANUARY 1982
The Committee's terms of reference as announced by the Secretary of State in answer to a parliamentary question on 23 December 1981:

1 For the time being and in the light of resources specified for Local Authority Higher Education in England by the Secretary of State after consultation with local authorities, to consider, on the basis of recommendations from the Board for Local Authority Higher Education, the academic provision to be made in institutions in selected fields as decided by the Committee.
2 To advise the Secretary of State, in respect of those fields, on the appropriate use of his powers with regard to the apportionment of the advanced further education pool and to the approval of advanced courses.
3 To monitor the implementation by local authorities and institutions of dispositions made by the Secretary of State in the light of this advice.
4 In formulating this advice, to contribute to a co-ordinated approach to provision, as necessary in relevant academic fields, between the local authority and the university, voluntary and direct grant sectors of higher education.
5 To undertake or commission such studies or to seek such information as appear necessary for the determination of this advice.

TERMS OF REFERENCE OF THE BOARD FOR LOCAL AUTHORITY HIGHER EDUCATION JANUARY 1982
The Board's terms of reference as announced by the Secretary of State in answer to a parliamentary question on 23 December 1981:

To receive instructions from and make recommendations to the Committee for Local Authority Higher Education in pursuit of the fulfilment of the Committee's Terms of Reference. In so doing, the Board will:

(a) establish such ad hoc groups as the Committee judges necessary to assist with aspects of this task;
(b) establish effective liaison with the university, voluntary and direct grant sectors of higher education, with appropriate validating and

professional bodies and, as necessary, with representatives of industry and commerce;

(c) secure advice from appropriate sources as necessary on the regional and local aspects of local authority education.

RECONSTITUTION OF THE NATIONAL ADVISORY BODY

A DES press notice (23/85) issued in January 1985 announced the reconstitution of the National Advisory Body for Local Authority Higher Education as the National Advisory Body for Public Sector Higher Education.

Education Secretary Sir Keith Joseph today announced the new membership and terms of reference of the National Advisory Body for Public Sector Higher Education (NAB) on its formal reconstitution on 1 February.

The NAB's terms of reference have been amended to reflect its new responsibilities for advising on provision in the voluntary sector and on capital provision.

Terms of Reference of the Committee

1 In the light of the resources specified for local authority higher education in England by the Secretary of State after consultation with the local authorities, and of the resources specified by him for the voluntary colleges, to consider on the basis of recommendations from the Board, the academic provision to be made in each of the institutions within the NAB's remit.

2 To advise the Secretary of State on the appropriate use of his powers with regard to the apportionment of the advanced further education pool, the allocation of resources for capital expenditure for local authority higher education, the allocation of resources to the voluntary colleges and the approval of advanced courses.

3 To monitor the implementation by local authorities and institutions of dispositions made by the Secretary of State in the light of this advice.

4 In formulating this advice, to contribute to a co-ordinated approach to provision, as necessary in relevant academic fields, between the local authority, voluntary, university and direct grant sectors of higher education and between the provision in England and that in other countries of the United Kingdom.

5 To undertake or commission such studies or to seek such information as appear necessary for the determination of such advice.

6 The institutions within the remit of the NAB are all the local authority maintained or assisted institutions of further education offering courses of advanced further education and the following voluntary colleges:

> Newman College
> Westhill College
> West Sussex Institute*
> Homerton College
> Christ Church College
> College of St Paul & St Mary

Chester College
Derbyshire College of Higher Education*
St Martin's College
Trinity & All Saints' College
Bishop Grosseteste College
Liverpool Institute of Higher Education
Roehampton Institute of Higher Education
St Mary's College
West London Institute*
De La Salle College
Westminster College
College of St Mark & St John
La Sainte Union College of Higher Education
King Alfred's College
College of Ripon and York St John

*Jointly maintained institutions

Terms of Reference of the Board

To receive instructions from and make recommendations to the Committee in pursuit of the fulfilment of the Committee's Terms of Reference. In so doing, the Board will:

(a) establish such ad hoc groups as the Committee judges necessary to assist with aspects of this task;
(b) in formulating recommendations for the voluntary colleges, consult the Voluntary Sector Consultative Council;
(c) establish effective liaison with the university and direct grant sectors of higher education, with appropriate validating, professional and accrediting bodies and, as necessary with representatives of industry, commerce and the professions; and with those concerned with the provision of higher education in the other countries of the United Kingdom;
(d) secure advice from appropriate sources as necessary on the regional and local aspects of higher education in the local authority and voluntary sectors of higher education.

Appendix B

Higher Education and the Needs of Society

A Joint statement by the National Advisory Body and the University Grants Committee, in which 'we' refers to both bodies, was published in 1984 as Chapter 2 in 'A Strategy for Higher Education in the Late 1980s and Beyond' (NAB 1984).

1   More than twenty years ago the Robbins Committee identified four objectives essential to the higher education system. These it described as: instruction in skills; promotion of the general powers of the mind; the advancement of learning; and the transmission of a common culture and common standards of citizenship. The meaning given to some of these terms and the context in which they might apply have changed since the time of the Robbins Report. Nevertheless, we believe they form an appropriate basis for considering the present and future role of higher education in our society.

2   Providing instruction in skills and promoting the powers of the mind remain the main teaching purposes of higher education. In carrying out this role higher education attempts to meet both the needs of the economy for highly skilled manpower and the aspirations of individuals for an educational experience which will provide for personal development and lead to a fulfilling and rewarding career. The faster pace of scientific, technological and economic change which our society now experiences has implications for the types of skill which higher education attempts to inculcate.

3   Specific knowledge quickly becomes outdated and the context in which it is applied rapidly changes. Initial higher education, particularly at diploma and first degree level, should therefore emphasise underlying intellectual scientific and technological principles rather than provide too narrow a specialist knowledge. The abilities most valued in industrial, commercial and professional life as well as in public and social administration are the transferable intellectual and personal skills. These include the ability to analyse complex issues, to identify the core of a problem and the means of solving it, to synthesise and integrate disparate elements, to clarify values, to make effective use of numerical and other information, to work co-operatively and constructively with others, and, above all perhaps, to communicate clearly both orally and in writing. A higher education system which provides its students with these skills is serving society well.

4   The world has changed since Robbins reported. The focus of initial higher education must now be broader and the recent increased emphasis on continuing education must be maintained and accelerated. Many commentators have written about a new industrial revolution, based on information technology, biotechnology and other scientific advances. The need for updating, refreshment, and re-orientation and for the development of new skills and attitudes is more pervasive, and in a sense more mundane. It affects for example the professions seeking to cope not only with technological advance, but also with changes in their legislative and regulatory framework; management and trades unions seeking to understand and adapt to their changing social and economic environment; those in the public services absorbing new ideas on the orientation and organisation of their work; and the unemployed seeking to re-enter the labour market in new fields of employment.

5   Continuing education needs to be fostered not only for its essential role in promoting economic prosperity but also for its contribution to personal development and social progress. It can renew personal confidence, regenerate the human spirit and restore a sense of purpose to people's lives through the cultivation of new interests. In short, both effective economic performance and harmonious social relationships depend on our ability to deal successfully with the changes and uncertainties which are now ever present in our personal and working lives. That is the primary role which we see for continuing education.

6   We have considered whether this increased emphasis on continuing education should be seen as a re-interpretation of Robbins' first two objectives or as a new objective. In view of the importance we attach to continuing education we see merit in emphasizing the establishment of a new objective rather than simply re-interpreting those enumerated over twenty years ago. This we would define as:

> the provision of continuing education in order to facilitate adjustment to technological, economic and social change and to meet individual needs for personal development.

7   In concentrating on the teaching functions of higher education the Robbins Committee's first two objectives answer in part the question 'What is higher education for?' They do not answer the question 'Who is higher education for?' The approach of the Robbins Committee to this question is enshrined in the famous axiom that courses of higher education should be available for all those who are qualified by ability and attainment to pursue them and who wish to do so. This has been the guiding principle of higher education planning for the past two decades.

8   We re-affirm the importance of access and the provision of opportunity. However, the Robbins axiom should be interpreted as broadly as possible, particularly in relation to the term 'qualified'. Essentially a student's qualification is used to form a judgement on his or her ability to benefit from a course. Yet evidence shows that school examinations such as 'A' levels are not always good predictors of achievement in higher education and that other qualities and

experience can be important determinants to success. We believe that
the Robbins axiom is more appropriately re-stated as 'courses of
higher education should be available for all those who are able to
benefit from them and who wish to do so'.

9　The third objective of the Robbins Committee refers to the
advancement of learning. The extension and application of knowledge are at the heart of the educational process: indeed, that process
is itself most vital when it partakes of the nature of discovery.
Moreover, through its research activity, higher education makes a
major contribution to the continued health of the nation's industry
and commerce. To curtail research would in the long run impoverish
the nation materially as well as culturally.

10　The language of Robbins's final objective − 'the transmission of a
common culture and common standards of citizenship' − may seem
somewhat dated nowadays when so much emphasis is placed on the
contribution which diverse cultures can make to the vitality and
strength of our society. Yet it is still true that there are common
values which education seeks to transmit and which help to give
society its cohesion and stability. These include the need to protect
the free expression and the testing of ideas, and the examination of
cases and arguments on their merits. In this sense the objective is
even more relevant in today's multi-cultural society than it was twenty
years ago. The Robbins Committee's own elaboration of the objective
indicates that the sentiments which underlie it still apply today. 'This
function, important at all times, is perhaps especially important in an
age that has set for itself the ideal of equality of opportunity. It is not
merely by providing places for students from all classes that this ideal
will be achieved, but also by providing, in the atmosphere of the
institutions in which the students live and work, influences that in
some measure compensate for any inequalities of home background.
These influences are not limited to the student population. Universities and colleges have an important role to play in the general cultural
life of the communities in which they are situated.'

11　The principle of access, which we have re-affirmed and re-
formulated above, is concerned with providing places for students
from different backgrounds and attempting to compensate for
previous inequalities. We would broaden it and include students not
only from different social classes, but also from different ethnic
groups. Moreover, opportunities for women must be as good as
opportunities for men. The principle is also concerned with the
relationship between each institution and its locality. It is as
important as ever that institutions should contribute to the cultural
life of their communities. In the world of the 1980s, it is equally
important to contribute to the economic, industrial and commercial
life of the locality.

12　A longer-term strategy must build on the strengths of the two sectors
of higher education and must maintain the present diversity of
provision. Full-time first degree courses will continue to be a major
activity of both universities and major public sector institutions.
Although most subjects of study are available in both sectors, we do

not consider that there is any general problem of duplication in view of the spread of institutions and of differences in the structure of courses and in the students attracted to them. Areas of excessive or inadequate provision will need to be considered by both sides of higher education together; so far as England is concerned, we intend to do it jointly. We would expect the universities to continue to be responsible for the bulk of postgraduate provision, particularly full-time courses and postgraduate work designed to prepare students for careers in research. The public sector should continue to provide the bulk of non-degree courses and of part-time courses. But where there is clear evidence of demand, institutions in either sector should not be prevented from introducing courses which arise from and are connected to their existing offerings.

13 For the public sector, continuing education has always been as important as the education of school-leavers. Universities have varied very much in their involvement. The expansion of continuing education which we believe to be necessary will offer a challenge to both sectors and should be based on their different experience and strengths. It must take account of the contribution of the Open University.

14 The general leadership of the universities in research work is recognized and reflected in the funding arrangements for the two sectors, but we agree that there is a legitimate research role for major public sector institutions, both to support and sustain teaching and as a contribution to the advancement and application of knowledge.

Appendix C

Towards a Strategy for Local Authority Higher Education in the Late 1980s and Beyond

The National Advisory Body put out a consultative document in May 1983.

INTRODUCTION

1 The National Advisory Body for Local Authority Higher Education is charged with advising the Secretary of State for Education and Science on the provision of higher education for nearly one third of a million students following over 10,000 courses in nearly 400 local authority colleges, and on the allocation of resources from the advanced further education pool in support of those courses. In addition to advice on the immediate impact of some of the Secretary of State's decisions, and on the current allocation of resources, it is engaged in a major planning exercise for 1984/85. It has also decided to review the longer-term strategies available to the system, and is publishing this consultative document as a step in that process.

2 The importance of higher education to society, and its significance as an investment in the future of individuals, and in the continued strength of industry, commerce, and the professions, means that no single simple line of development can be followed by the system. The range of provision made by local authority colleges is wider than that in any other sector of higher education, and the complexities of the spectrum of level, subject content, and mode of attendance are such as to make generalisations dangerous. The scope and scale of the provision made may be summarised as follows: over half the students study full-time; the courses cover a wide spectrum of professional and vocational areas, at sub-degree and higher technician levels, at degree level, and in postgraduate and post-experience study and research (research policy for the sector is not examined in this paper, but is the subject of a consultative report issued earlier this year by NAB). The characteristic features of the sector lie in its variety, its flexibility, its responsiveness to the local, regional, and national needs of industry, business and the public services, and its openness in terms of non-traditional access. About 150,000 students are on degree courses, many of whom are mature entrants (about one-third of all full-time students), and a significant minority have come in without formal qualifications. A high proportion of the students are preparing directly for entry to professional life, and seeking to develop particular skills as well as their general abilities; and over half the

students are following sub-degree and higher technician courses, so that the provision of degree courses with entry at eighteen plus for the holders of appropriate GCE 'A' level qualifications, although significant, is simply not of itself an adeqate picture of the sector.

3   It is now over fifteen years since the White Paper on Polytechnics (DES 1966), and nearly a decade since radical changes were imposed on the then teacher training colleges. The CNAA is engaged in re-defining its own role in the light of its successful experience, while TEC and BEC have merged: all three have existed in their present forms since 1973/74. The last major reports on higher education (Robbins 1963) and on day-release (Henniker-Heaton 1964) are nearly twenty years old. Aspects of the system have been considered since then, particularly in the series of DES publications beginning with, and consequent upon, the 1972 Education White Paper (DES 1972). Now that the 1984/85 NAB planning exercise is firmly under way, it is appropriate to look beyond the short-term necessities to the later years of the decade, with the intention of mapping out a preferred strategy (or strategies) which might influence and shape the sector beyond 1985, while progressively informing the decisions to be made for that and subsequent years.

4   NAB is quite clear that the questions addressed in this document cannot be answered for the local authority colleges in isolation. It is charged under its terms of reference to contribute to a co-ordinated approach to provision between the local authority and the university, voluntary and direct grant sectors of higher education. Accordingly, many of the questions raised in this paper arise across the whole system of higher education in the United Kingdom, and may give rise to observations about the provision in the other sectors: in identifying some of the issues, NAB is anxious that they should be examined in terms of their educational merit, as much as in the light of the identified needs of industry, commerce, the professions and the public service, and that responses should neither be sought solely from, nor limited in their contents to, the local authority sector of higher education. In consequence, others beside NAB will be interested in the responses to this paper: in accordance with its terms of reference, NAB will keep them informed of the views it receives, and hopes that they will find this useful. NAB will welcome comments on any or all of the possibilities set out later in this document, which should be sent to reach it by not later than 31 December 1983.

BACKGROUND

5   Some of the characteristic features of local authority provision are currently being questioned. It is said that the sector is not as responsive to employment needs as it should be: yet it is difficult at the system-wide level to discern clearly what these needs are. NAB has set up an Industry Group to make an informed contribution to this debate in due course. The proportion of students in the sector following science and engineering courses has tended to decrease, while the proportion following courses in the business and commer-

cial area has increased: this change has certainly reflected both student demand and locally perceived employment demand, but it cannot be said to have been planned on an overall basis. The flexibility of response of the colleges is said to be inhibited by an excess of bureaucratic controls: the move to programme planning represents one possible route to achieving greater flexibility. The funding mechanisms are said to militate against the enhanced provision of non-full-time modes of provision: hence the changes in this area in respect of the 1983-84 pool allocations.

6 At the same time, resources for higher education are being reduced (reflecting both a governmental will to reduce public expenditure and a planning assumption that there will be fewer students), and the number of students is still growing (probably reflecting both the peaking of the eighteen plus age group and the social pressure arising from increasing unemployment). In the absence of an acceptable rationale, the system is acting in such a way as to reduce the effective annual unit of resource per student: the balance of provision is not adjusting itself to take account of these effects: and the risk of an unacceptably poor quality of provision grows larger. The government and various interest groups in society are simultaneously making the case for increased access to, and provision of, higher education, whether in specific areas (information technology), to increase industrial and commercial competence and versatility (PICKUP), to enhance individual opportunities (comparison with European competitors and defence of the historic Robbins principle), or for social reasons (unemployment).

7 The view taken of the role of higher education in society inevitably rests explicitly on, or assumes, a view about that society itself. It is not the purpose of this paper to seek to identify or to evaluate alternative economic futures for the country, nor to engage in speculation about the future shape of British society. Nevertheless, such issues are relevant: the continued presence of structural unemployment, especially of young people, must have an effect on the totality of the secondary and tertiary education systems, as must the extent to which education, particularly some aspects of higher education, is seen as being on the one hand a consumer of resources or on the other hand a necessary precursor to and investment in industrial regeneration and economic growth. Similarly, such views inform comparisons with the provision of, and rates of participation in, higher education in other countries; for this and other reasons, it is not easy to make proper comparisons. The latest figures published by the DES (in Report on Education 99) (DES 1983) show higher education new entrant participation rates (calculated on an OECD basis) ranging from 19.2 per cent (FRG) to 42.8 per cent (USA), with France at 27.7 per cent, the UK at 31 per cent and Japan at 39.2 per cent.

8 Nevertheless, participation rates are an important indicator of the national investment in higher education: during the years 1978/79 to 1981/82 the age specific participation rate for entry to higher education in Great Britain (as a percentage of 18-year-olds) rose from 12.4 per cent to 13.2 per cent. Although the picture of higher

education centred on the eighteen plus entrant to a full-time course, typically of three years' duration, has never been more than partial, demographic changes in the eighteen plus age group have been a major determinant of the size of the system, and a less than adequate proxy for measuring resource needs. Thus, over the same period of time, the number of mature entrants also rose, to a total of over 36,000. In the absence of additional resources, and unless the reducing sums made available by the Government are used differently, these levels of participation must fall.

9 Considerable attention is focused on the demographic factors: these can be presented in a number of ways, and with the exception of gross data (births, sizes of age groups) require some care in interpretation, since assumptions have to be made about staying-on rates, and about qualifying rates. Current DES figures (April 1983) show a decline in the school-leaving cohort from a current figure (the highest ever) of over 760,000 to some 580,000 in 1990/91: this reflects a decline in (legitimate) births from 813,000 in 1964 to 720,000 in 1970 (and to 514,000 in 1977). Over the same period, however, the estimate of births in social classes I and II rose from 136,000 in 1964 to 148,000 in 1970 (and declined again to 142,000 in 1977). In consequence, the number of persons forecast to obtain two or more GCE 'A' level passes (allowance being made for qualifications gained in further education) falls from 122,000 (current peak value) to only 108,000 in 1990/91 (and to 94,000 in 1995/96). These figures, and their implications (both social and financial) require careful consideration: more details are available in DES Statistical Bulletin 6/83. Potential demand figures are analysed in DES Report on Education 99 (April 1983).

SOME ASPECTS OF THE SYSTEM

10 It has long been the case, in reality, that the higher education system (especially the local authority sector) has responded to a variety of planning imperatives. The following paragraphs summarise, by way of background, some of the more important aspects of the system. They are by no means mutually exclusive, but all have at different times exerted a powerful influence on provision.

11 One view (often identified with the Robbins principle) adopts as its starting point the individual's access to the system, and proceeds (in a developed form) to consider society's demands ('informed student demand'). It recognises the argument from missed opportunity (the Open University), which it sees as also a loss of potential to society; and as originally understood (courses of higher education should be available to those qualified to undertake them, wishing to do so and capable of benefiting from them) does not presuppose location, duration or subject specificity. Only by custom has the three-year eighteen plus degree course come to be identified wih this view. Moreover, the approach has never really satisfactorily incorporated the different concepts of part-time and continuing education; it can be very simply categorised as a model of initial full-time higher education; its contribution to the system has been to concentrate attention on individual opportunity.

12　The view of the qualified professional is a rather older one: traditionally it emphasised the integration of practice with college-based study and was perhaps at its strongest in the traditional route to qualification as a professional engineer. This perspective encouraged part-time and sandwich modes of study, did not accept initial full-time higher education as satisfactorily completing the educative process and provided a series of progressive stages through which an individual could advance as opportunity and aptitude allowed. It is a matter of regret that so many professional bodies have moved towards an over-emphasis on the three-year degree course as the (only) entry route to professional status, thereby increasing the tendency to disregard the educational and social advantages of other modes.

13　Identified needs for qualified manpower have always played a part in the planning of the system, and in its responses. In its simplest form, a college has responded to the identified needs of an employer and provided a tailor-made course: at the national level medicine and teacher training are good examples. Over the years, a number of reports have examined aspects of this approach in detail: in general (and over-simplifying) they have stressed the need for a greater weight to be given to technician-level higher education. Seen from the viewpoint of industry and commerce, the case has repeatedly been made for higher education that is more immediately vocationally specific, and of shorter initial duration.

14　Continuing education is now seen as very important, and places its emphasis on the changing needs of the world of work, and therefore of the qualified individual. Hence it leads to a greater provision of short-mode courses, taken typically in 'mid'-career, and implying − because initial higher education is no longer a once for all, career-long, investment − that initial courses in higher education may not, perhaps, need to be quite so long as some are at the moment. It is important to note, however, that in this model the total of higher education is not necessarily less: it is differently spread over a lifetime and, possibly, differently funded from the traditional model. Moreover, considerations of access to higher education, especially in relation to a reasonable spread of provision throughout the country, are emphasized when seen from this viewpoint.

STUDENT ACCESS AND PURPOSES

15　The objectives of an individual student entering upon initial or post experience/qualification higher education may, or may not, match tidily those implied by one or another of the viewpoints described above. There is no a priori reason to think that they will, and considerable anecdotal evidence to suggest that student motivation changes over the duration of a course. Some features do however seem clear: most students embark on courses of initial higher education expecting to gain a formal qualification that will (directly or otherwise) enhance their employment prospects. Similarly, the majority of those embarking on courses expect that if they perform sufficiently well, and are so inclined, they will be able to progress to further study. The notions of progression, formal qualification, and career benefit are firmly embedded.

16 The components of employment relevance and formal qualification are also present in the minds of most students on (long) post-qualification/experience courses. To assert this is not to devalue the cultural benefits gained by students in higher education, nor to deny that some enter it for wholly other reasons, and without any obvious thought of employment aim or advantage. Rather it is to seek to identify some of the features of the system seen as important by those entering it. The degree of importance will naturally vary with the age and previous experience of the potential entrant; in particular, experience of unemployment will colour the student's approach, especially if the course is seen as offering a second chance, or a retraining opportunity in an area where traditional employment openings are in decline. On the other hand, some students will always seek higher education primarily for its personal benefits at a time of increased or enforced leisure, whether resulting from retirement or otherwise.

17 The importance of progression and of formal qualifications is recognizable also at the point of entry to higher education. The concern of local authorities for higher education springs partly from their concern for the follow-on from school, and also for the proper articulation of non-advanced further education with higher education. Students are prepared for entry to higher education in both schools and colleges, and a qualification-based system of entry to initial higher education depends very much on the future of examinations which are also relied on for the effective certification of those leaving schools and further education colleges for work. Possible changes in the nature and structure of these examinations are necessarily one aspect of the work of those who are involved in planning and providing higher education.

18 Although it is not the function of this paper to do more than identify some of these issues, many of which are and have been the subject of more extensive consideration elsewhere, they impact on one of the central features of the present discussion − the level of demand. Traditional measures of demand are rooted largely in estimates of the qualifications and expectations of the proxy cohort, and these measures are under strain in several different ways.

19 First the question arises as to whether the reduction in opportunity consequent upon current expenditure cuts is having a differential, and unintended, effect *within* the traditional entrant group. Alongside general concern about the effects of the cuts in university provision, there is seen to be a particular need to ensure that access and re-entry to higher education by women and girls is not differentially eroded.

20 Secondly, there is concern about the access to higher education of non-traditional groups (predominantly identified either by social class or by ethnic origin) which, it is argued, has always been too low, and is likely to become lower as a result of the cuts. In this connection, the idea of progression is allied with an argument which suggests that

some non-traditional entrants are discouraged by the need to commit themselves, on entry to initial higher education, to what are seen as lengthy periods of study before any qualification can be obtained.

21 Thirdly, the generally accepted need for a greater provision of post-experience courses coincides with a period in which the age cohorts from which the mature entrants to higher education are drawn will increase for at least the next two decades. These strains will affect the system in different ways, and on different timescales, but they are all relevant to the determination of a long-term strategy.

POSSIBLE COURSES OF ACTION

22 In his letter of guidance to NAB (February 1983), the Secretary of State indicated that for 1984/85 he hoped that 'without neglect to the pattern of student demand, priority will be accorded to the scientific and technological provision of value to industry, to the operational needs of industry, commerce and the professions, and to meeting the future needs of employers more generally, not least at technician level.' In addition, in relation to the longer term, he went on to say, 'I hope, however, that it will be possible to look further ahead to what kind of AFE provision, including appropriate provision for research, will be required for the later eighties and nineties. It is important that traditional assumptions be questioned, and I welcome the NAB's debate on possible future patterns of provision. I hope that this debate will include discussions with the UGC on whether the trend towards a homogeneous higher education system with the precedence given to 3-year first degrees at the expense of other more vocationally orientated courses is in the best future interests of the nation. As the 18-year-old population declines, it will become increasingly important for the local authority higher education sector to develop its existing ability to cater for a range of ages through a variety of modes of attendance at different levels of study.'

23 On educational and social grounds questions about access must be answered, and related simultaneously to answers to questions about the needs of individuals, and of the world of work. The discussion must take place recognising both that the proxy measure of size (the eighteen plus age group) will decline, and that real resource constraints exist now and will continue. The views described above, and the subsequent paragraphs, identify questions about the content, mode, and duration of courses, particularly initial courses, of higher education.

24 The reality is that a variety of courses of action is open to the system, and must indeed be pursued in an appropriate combination if the problems already identified are to be effectively tackled. It is in relation to the balance between possible courses of action, and to the emphases to be placed on them, that the questions in this paper are addressed.

25 There are questions about the best use of academic staff and buildings, and about related pedagogic matters. In the local authority sector, the length and structure of the academic and teaching year and week are (formally) well defined, the average size of classes has

long been largely determined by the way in which the approval of
courses system has been operated, and for many courses traditional
patterns of teaching involve (by comparative standards) relatively
high figures of hours of formal instruction. Not a great deal of
attention has in general been paid to distance learning techniques,
computer assisted and other self-paced learning methods; and in
relation to this and other aspects of the work of the colleges,
insufficient thought may have been given to the most effective
balance of non-teaching and academic staff. Accordingly:

A   Should the existing length and structure of the academic year be
    changed? And if so, how?
B   Assuming no other change in existing patterns, should the
    average size of classes be increased? And if so, by how much?
C   Similarly, should students be taught for fewer hours? And if so,
    with what balancing provision in libraries, study space, etc?
D   More generally, should greater use be made of distance learning
    techniques, and of computer assisted learning and allied
    methods? And if so, to what effect?
E   Is there a general case for altering the balance between teaching
    and support staff? And if so, to what effect?

26 Questions of student support involve consideration of awards and of
    whether the students pay fees, and more widely of such possibilities as
    paid education leave: the present structure can be seen as favouring
    (initial) full-time entrants at the expense of part-time students and
    those returning to higher education. Broadly speaking, fees for
    full-time (home) students are fixed on the basis that they represent an
    element of the funding that will flow to the institution from the public
    purse by one route or another, and fees for part-time students on a
    pro-rata basis, and on the assumption that they are likely to be met by
    some form of sponsorship. In neither case is the self-financing
    student a significant element in the calculations. Awards are available
    without limitation of numbers or (very nearly) of subject of study, but
    only in relation to initial courses of full-time and sandwich higher
    education. Moreover, within the awards sceme, there is effective
    financial support for the widespread belief that it is, in principle,
    desirable that students should live away from home: many institu-
    tions accept without considering its justification their ability to recruit
    students without regard to their home address. Discussion about the
    possible introduction of a student loans scheme represents one
    response to some of the implied questions, but any major change
    seems likely to be possible in practice only if and when a substantial,
    but theoretically temporary, increase in expenditure is possible.
    Therefore:

F   Does the balance (of student support) between initial and post
    initial entrants, and between full-time and part-time students
    require modification? And if so, how, e.g. by modifications of the
    student support arrangements?

G   Is the present (home student) fee structure acceptable? And if not, what modifications are desirable?

H   More specifically, should the present (unrestricted) provision for students to live and study away from home be continued without modification? And if not, bearing in mind the large capital investment in student residential facilities, what changes are practicable?

I   Are there other related issues (such as PEL) which NAB should address with a high degree of priority?

27 Some changes are possible within the present structure and pattern of courses. An increase in access on the part of non-traditional groups, and the further development of continuing education, might call for greater mobility between levels of work, and/or for the introduction of an effective credit transfer mechanism. Professional and qualifying bodies might need to review the extent of their insistence on entry via full-time courses, and their tendency to ask for degrees instead of diplomas, and for diplomas instead of certificates. Depending on the view taken about the future of British society, the balance between general (and cultural) courses (the DipHE, liberal arts degrees) and more specifically vocational courses (BTEC diplomas, engineering degrees) could be changed. Consequently:

J   Is an effective (national) credit transfer system needed? And if so, how might it most effectively be developed?

K   Are the possibilities of progression between levels of higher education, and particularly between sub-degree level courses, adequately defined? And if not, what action is required?

L   More particularly, is the commitment of time (i.e. duration) on initial entry to full-time higher education an obstacle to non-traditional entrants?

M   Should the present balance between degree (3 and 4-year courses) and diploma (mostly 2-year courses) courses be varied? And if so, to what extent?

N   Within any such view, what should be the balance between general courses, and more specifically vocational ones?

O   Do respondents have any observations to make on the practices of professional and qualifying bodies?

28 Other possible changes are more radical, and would involve changes in patterns of working, and/or in the generally accepted consensus about appropriate modes of provision. Nevertheless, examples exist within Great Britain of qualifications awarded after shorter periods of study (in terms of calendar years) than is customary, and of the use of the ordinary (rather than the honours) course as the normal initial qualification. Taken together, and considered alongside other possibilities that have been advocated but not tried out, questions such as the following arise:

P   Should the ordinary degree be more widely used (as in Scotland)?

Q Should existing (mainly honours) degree courses be shortened in length by using, for example, a four-term year?

R Should some institutions offer ordinary degrees in two (calendar) years?

29 The questions listed in the previous paragraphs are set out in a very simple way: NAB recognises that they are not in practice simple, and that the answers to them are not necessarily single ones. To seek to balance answers to questions about individual access and employment related needs within resource constraints is neither new nor easy. It is desirable, however, that NAB should attempt the exercise in the interest of the sector it is intended to serve. One possible synthesis offers itself, if access is to be maximised while allowing employment-related needs to influence provision to a greater extent. If more students took all, or some, of their higher education part-time; if more students lived at home; if a greater proportion of initial courses of full-time higher education were shorter rather than longer: then conflicting demands on the system could be met.

30 This is, of course, only one synthesis: there are many others, which respondents may wish to identify. An obvious alternative, not automatically to be ruled out, is to continue with the present pattern of provision but – in the absence of more resources – to reduce access. Or, if the balance of courses is not to be changed, but access is to be protected, patterns of working involving a different academic year and greater utilisation of teaching accommodation (presumably at some cost) might be introduced. The circle cannot be squared: given the resource constraints, then unless the pattern of provision is modified, the alternative to a reduction in access is a wholly unacceptable deterioration in quality. It is true that the financial analysis of alternative approaches is complex, even when the prior educational/employment questions have been thought through. It rests on a variety of assumptions about the nature of the provision, the extent to which students reside away from home, and the relative costs of tuition and student support within the grants system. Nevertheless it can be undertaken.

31 It is interesting to note that the possibilities are also being studied by others. Thus, for example, a proportionately greater provision of higher education on the two-year full-time mode (whether diploma or ordinary degree) could release resources sufficient both to meet the needs of continuing education and to offer higher education places to a higher proportion not only of the eighteen plus age group but also of potential mature students. This option, which seen from a purely individual perspective offers more individuals the opportunity of access to higher education, is currently being examined both by the Leverhulme study, and by the CNAA in its examination of its future pattern of awards.

32 The asking of questions such as those already listed brings with it disadvantages. If the local authority sector were to be uniquely identified with any possible outcome, there could be fears of a 'second class' status for the sector. If, as suggested, the questions are faced

across the entire higher education system, but changes take place only in some institutions within it, similar fears will be voiced. This is not the intention: some changes are probably inevitable, others desirable. Moreover, the questions will not go away. Indeed, there may well be additional points to be raised. The last question to be listed must therefore be:

S   Are there other points relating to the issues raised in this paper which respondents wish to make?

CONCLUSION

33   NAB does not believe that even if a consensus view emerges from the answers to the questions identified in this paper changes can be brought about with great rapidity, particularly if they are radical in their nature. What is needed now is an open debate about possible changes, and about the courses of action available to the system and to the sectors and institutions within it. The National Advisory Body therefore invites comments on the ideas canvassed in this paper, and responses to the questions identified above.

Appendix D

Keble – a Pioneering College

The University of Oxford is a federation of colleges: membership of the university can only be achieved through membership of one of the colleges. Keble, the twenty-first Oxford college, was founded at a time when the university was achieving its maturity as the model for contemporary higher education in the western world. Whilst treasuring what is best of Oxford's medieval traditions – such as the outstanding collection of medieval manuscripts in the College library – Keble is also a pioneering college, seeking in every generation to be in the forefront of the Oxford quest for excellence.

The nineteenth century was an era of change and reform for Oxford. The university was to a large extent recreated and redirected through the work of a succession of Royal Commissions and the ideas of certain visionaries: the saintly John Keble, author of 'The Christian Year', founder of the Tractarian movement and originator of the pastoral role of the Oxford tutor; the liberal statesman William Gladstone who strove to ensure that places and positions at Oxford should depend upon merit, rather than rank, privilege or vested interest; Mark Pattison who insisted upon the importance of scholarship and research in the modern university; Benjamin Jowett, creator of the Oxford tradition of providing the nation with a succession of men fit to undertake the highest offices; and Cecil Rhodes, the imperialist who founded the system of Rhodes scholarships and ensured that Oxford would be an international university.

Keble is one of the most important and lasting outcomes of this ferment of change and renewal. Founded in 1870 as a permanent memorial to the Oxford Movement, the college received its inspiration alike from Tractarians such as Keble and Pusey and from nineteenth-century liberals like Gladstone (the Prime Minister) and Lord Shaftesbury who shared 'the democratic feeling of the century, which desired that the advantages of the best education should be shared by all'. It was to be 'an institution in which young men now debarred from university education might be trained in simple and religious habits'. The college now happily admits both men and women, and permits and protects the free exercise of religion. The ideas of its founders can still be recognized in the unpretentious friendliness and social diversity of its members and in a devotion to human values and 'the high culture of the mind'.

The first Warden, Edward Talbot, who also played a major part in the development of women's colleges in Oxford, created a college where students could live economically, eating at the common table in the great

Hall, and living in modest rooms in the magnificent buildings of William Butterfield. The success of the college can be seen by the way in which so many of the ideals of its founders (admission by merit, the value of tutorial teaching, domestic economy, for example) have become standard practice in Oxford (and elsewhere). Over the period of a century or more Keble has played its part in providing 'a succession of persons duly qualified for the service of God in church and state'. It has attracted and nurtured a number of Rhodes scholars and other students from overseas: two of the present Tutorial Fellows are citizens of the USA.

Today, the college is again a pioneer in Oxford. Having admitted women to membership in 1980, the Governing Body undertook a thorough review of admissions procedures in 1982 and devised the 'Keble Scheme' which, when it was announced to other colleges, precipitated a general intercollegiate debate, and the ultimate adoption by all colleges of a reformed system for admissions in 1985. As a special contribution towards the university's research effort, the college has sought to develop a limited programme of short-term Junior Research Fellowships, and has recently created three new tutorial posts in science and engineering in as many years. And in 1983 Keble devised and inaugurated a scheme whereby junior members can consult old members of the college about careers. This concern for careers-advice and placement is now being further developed in conjunction with the University Appointments Committee.

Keble has set itself the task of redefining and recreating in modern terms the essentials of an Oxford collegiate education — admission on merit to an international community, tutorial teaching, scholarship and the ultimate purpose of service to the nation in the world of employment.

References

ABRC (1983) *Report of a Working Party of the Advisory Board for the Research Councils on the Support given by Research Councils for In-house and University Research*

Aelfric *Lives of Three English Saints* ed. G.I. Needham 1966

Auden, W.H. (1966) *Collected Shorter Poems 1927-57*

Austen, Jane (1813) *Pride and Prejudice*

The Butler Act. The 1944 Education Act

Campbell, Roy (1982) *Selected Poems* ed. Peter Alexander

CNAA (1974) *Charter and Statutes*

CNAA (1979) *Developments in Partnership in Validation*

CNAA (1983) *Development of CNAA Undergraduate Awards* A Discussion Paper

DES (1956) *Technical Education* White Paper, Cmnd 9703

DES (1966) *A Plan for Polytechnics and Other Colleges: Higher Education in the Further Education System* White Paper, Cmnd 3006

DES (1967) *Notes for Guidance on the Government and Academic Organisation of Polytechnics* Administrative Memorandum 8/67

DES (1972) *Education: A Framework for Expansion* White Paper, Cmnd 5174

DES (1980) *Further Education Student Record* (annual collection)

DES (1982) *Circular 5/82: The Approval of Advanced Courses*

DES (1983) *Report on Education No 99*

DES (1983) *Statistical Bulletin 6/83*

DES (1984) *Report on Education No 100*

Donne, John *Poetical Works* ed. H.J.C. Grierson 1933

Donne, John *The Sermons of John Donne* University of Chicago 1984

Engineering Council (1984) *Standards and Routes to Registration. Policy Statement 1984*

The Franks Report (1966) *Report of Commission of Enquiry 1966. The Franks Report on the University of Oxford* OUP

Goodlad, Sinclair (Ed.)(1983) *Economies of Scale in Higher Education* SRHE

The Government's Expenditure Plans 1984-85 to 1986-87 White Paper, Cmnd 9143

Henniker-Heaton, C. (1964) *Report on Day Release*

Keble, John (1827) *The Christian Year*

Keble College Record (1980)

King Alfred's West-Saxon Version of Gregory's *Pastoral Care* ed. H.Sweet 1871

The Kneale Report (1965) *The Committee on the Structure of the First and Second Public Examinations (1965). University of Oxford* OUP

Langland, William (c 1380) *The Vision of Piers Plowman* ed. A.V.C. Schmidt 1978

The Leverhulme Report (1983) *Excellence in Diversity* SRHE

NAB (1983) *Towards a Strategy for Local Authority Higher Education in the Late 1980s and Beyond: A Consultative Document*

NAB (1983) *The Funding of Research Activity: A Discussion Document*

NAB (1984) *A Strategy for Higher Education in the Late 1980s and Beyond*

The Oakes Report (1978) *Report of the Working Group on the Management of Higher Education in the Maintained Sector under the Chairmanship of Mr G.J. Oakes MP* Cmnd 7130

Oldham, Geoffrey (Ed.)(1982) *The Future of Research* SRHE

Orwell, George (1949) *Nineteen Eighty-Four*

Oxford Review of Education (1982) Vol.8, No.3

Oxford Review of Education (1985) Vol.11, No.1

Pirsig, R.M. (1974) *Zen and the Art of Motorcycle Maintenance*

The Robbins Report (1963) *Report of the Committee on Higher Education under the Chairmanship of Lord Robbins* Cmnd 2154

Robinson, Ken (Ed.)(1982) *The Arts and Higher Education* SRHE

Sainte-Marie, Buffie (1971) *The Seeds of Brotherhood* Vanguard VSD 79250

Scott, Peter (1980-85 passim) *The Times Higher Education Supplement*

Snow, C.P. (1934) *The Search*

Snow, C.P. (1959) *The Two Cultures* (The Rede Lecture)

Williams, Gareth and Blackstone, Tessa (1983) *Response to Adversity* SRHE

Yeats, W.B. (1933) *Collected Poems*

Index

marxism   6
mathematics   22, 76, 80, 92
medicine   6, 75, 79, 89, 119
Milton, John   35
modular degrees   12, 25

National Advisory Body   ix, 17, 19,
    24-32, 34, 44-50, 51-55, 56-62,
    63-65, 66-68, 69-72, 73-76, 78-81,
    84-85, 89, 91, 94-95, 96-101, 103,
    105, 106, 108-110, 111-114, 115-
    125
National Council for Technological
    Awards   9
nautical studies   26
non-advanced further
    education   28, 45, 47, 49, 55, 57,
    63, 69, 75, 85, 94, 95, 120
North East London Polytechnic   51

Oakes Report   26
objectives (*see* aims)
Open University   10, 63, 95, 114,
    118
Orwell, George   51-52, 55
overseas students   25
Oxford University   33-39, 40-43, 44,
    64, 82, 83-84, 103-104, 126-127

Paradise Lost   35
Pattison, Mark   126
Paul, The Apostle   90
peer-group validation   13, 59, 70
performing arts   12
pharmacy   26
philosophy   5, 13, 76, 92
physics   76
Piers Plowman   3
Pirsig, R.M.   96
Polytechnic Central Admissions
    Scheme   82, 87
Popper, Karl   41
popular culture   5
professions   81, 98-99, 119, 123

quality   3, 10, 14, 22, 31, 49, 53, 57,
    63, 64, 68, 69, 71, 74, 85-86, 92,
    95, 96-102, 105, 117, 124

rate of change   49
regional advisory councils   49

regional planning   26, 28, 48, 62,
    64, 69, 74, 77
research   29, 36, 38, 45, 51, 52, 54,
    57, 60-61, 62, 70, 71
resources   7, 14, 17, 22, 27, 29, 31,
    35, 42, 49, 52-53, 56, 58, 67, 79,
    95, 99, 117, 124
responsiveness   12-13, 25, 30-31,
    57, 66-68, 69, 105-106, 115
Rhodes, Cecil   126
Robbins Report   9, 16, 20, 25, 30,
    52, 57, 67, 68, 71, 73, 79, 83

SRHE Leverhulme Report   16, 20,
    56-62, 63, 67, 72, 83, 85, 124
sandwich study   25, 29, 45, 69, 74,
    77, 87, 119
Saroyan, William   103, 107
Schumacher, Christian   46
science   22, 30-31, 41-43, 73, 75, 77,
    79, 84, 116, 127
Scott, Peter   76
seamless web   28, 51, 54, 57, 94
service disciplines   76-77, 79
Sheffield Polytechnic   6
Slee, Peter   83
Snow, C.P.   75, 90
sociology   5, 76
specialization   57, 59, 67, 76, 83, 111
standards   14-16, 22, 52, 107
Stevenson, R.L.   12, 91
structuralism   6
student awards   69, 72, 75, 81, 82,
    122
student demand   6, 30-31, 52, 80,
    82, 84
student numbers   50, 52-53, 54, 117
student/staff ratios   30, 53
subject boards   9-16, 48

Talbot, Edward   126
teacher training   22, 25, 26, 28, 45,
    57, 70-71, 75, 119
teaching   22, 27, 29, 33, 36, 38, 45,
    60, 69, 88, 112
technology   30-31, 76, 77, 79-80, 84
television   5-7
tenure   61, 65, 70
textile technology   26
Thames Polytechnic   8
theology   5

The Society for Research into Higher Education

The Society for Research into Higher Education exists to encourage and co-ordinate research and development in all aspects of higher education. It thus draws to public attention both the need for research and development and the needs of the research community. Its income is derived from subscriptions, and from research or other specific grants. It is wholly independent. Its corporate members are universities, polytechnics, institutes of higher education, research institutions and professional and governmental bodies. Its individual members are teachers and researchers, administrators and students. Members are found in all parts of the world and the Society regards its international work as amongst its most important activities.

The Society discusses and comments on policy, organizes conferences and sponsors research. Under the imprint SRHE & NFER-NELSON it is a specialist publisher of research, having over 30 titles in print. It also publishes Studies in Higher Education (three times a year), Higher Education Abstracts (three times a year), International Newsletter (twice a year), a Bulletin (six times a year), and jointly with the Committee for Research into Teacher Education (CRITE) Evaluation Newsletter (twice a year).

The Society's committees, study groups and local branches are run by members, with help from a small secretariat, and aim to provide a forum for discussion. Some of the groups, at present the Teacher Education Study Group and the Staff Development Group, have their own subscriptions and organization, as do some Regional Branches. The Governing Council, elected by members, comments on current issues and discusses policies with leading figures in politics and education. The Society organizes seminars on current research for officials of the DES and other ministries, and is in touch with bodies in Britain such as the CNAA, NAB, CVCP, UGC and the British Council; and with sister-bodies overseas. Its current research projects include one on the relationship between entry qualifications and degree results, directed by Prof. W.D. Furneaux (Brunel) and one on 'Questions of Quality' directed by Prof. G.C. Moodie (York).

The Society's annual conferences take up central themes, viz. 'Education for the Professions' (1984, with the help and support of DTI, UNESCO and many professional bodies), 'Continuing Education' (1985, organized in collaboration with Goldsmiths' College, the Open University and the University of Surrey, with advice from the DES and the CBI), 'Standards and criteria in HE' (1986). Joint conferences are held, viz. 'Cognitive Processes' (1985, with the Cognitive Psychology Section of the BPS), on the DES 'Green Paper' (1985, with The Times Higher Education Supplement) and on 'Information Technology' (1986, with the Council for Educational Technology). For some of the Society's conferences, special studies are commissioned in advance, as 'Precedings'.

Members receive free of charge the Society's Abstracts, annual conference proceedings (or 'Precedings'), and Bulletin and International Newsletter, and may buy SRHE & NFER-NELSON books at booksellers' discount. Corporate members receive the Society's journal Studies in Higher Education free, individuals at a heavy discount. They may also obtain Evaluation Newsletter and certain other journals at discount, including the NFER Register of Educational Research.

Further information may be obtained from the Society for Research into Higher Education, At the University, Guildford GU2 5XH, UK.